I0703011

1.

-- 1

Summary..4

Chapter 2 7

Chapter 3 10

Chapter 1: Introduction to Yoga for Politicians 12

Chapter 2: Understanding Stress and Leadership.......21

Chapter 3: Foundations of Yoga Practice...................30

Chapter 4: Yoga Poses for Physical Stamina and Health 40

Chapter 5: Breathing Techniques for Emotional Resilience 50

Chapter 6: Meditation Practices for Mental Clarity ...59

Chapter 7: Managing Public Speaking Anxiety 68

Chapter 8: Cultivating Empathy and Patience in Governance..78

Chapter 9: Ethical Alignment and Good Governance 87

Chapter 10: Creating a Culture of Wellness within Political Institutions..97

Chapter 11: Overcoming Challenges to Consistent Practice 107

Chapter 12: Short Yoga Breaks for Busy Schedules 116

Chapter 13: Advanced Techniques for Seasoned Practitioners 125

Chapter 14: Navigating Complex Negotiations with Clarity 134

Chapter 15: Leading with Wisdom and Compassion 143

Chapter 16: Ethical Leadership in Times of Crisis ..152

Chapter 17: Towards a Future of Sustainable Leadership 161

Synopsis..170

2.

3.

4.

5.

6.

7.

8.

9.

10.

11.

12.

13.

14.

15.

16.

17.

18.

19.

20.

21.

22.

Summary

Chapter 1: Introduction to Yoga for Politicians

4

1.1 The Need for Balance in Political Life

4

1.2 Overview of Yoga's Benefits for Leaders

7

1.3 The Journey Ahead

9

Chapter 2: Understanding Stress and Leadership

12

2.1 The Impact of Stress on Decision-Making

12

2.2 Leadership Challenges in the Political Arena

15

2.3 How Yoga Offers Solutions

18

Chapter 3: Foundations of Yoga Practice

22

3.1 History and Philosophy of Yoga

22

3.2 Key Principles and Ethics of Yoga

24

3.3 Establishing a Personal Practice

27

Chapter 4: Yoga Poses for Physical Stamina and Health

31

4.1 Essential Poses for Energy and Strength

31

4.2 Poses for Flexibility and Endurance

33

4.3 Recovery and Restorative Practices

36

Chapter 5: Breathing Techniques for Emotional Resilience

40

5.1 Understanding Pranayama

40

5.2 Breathing Exercises for Stress Management

43

5.3 Integrating Breathwork into Daily Routines

45

Chapter 6: Meditation Practices for Mental Clarity

49

6.1 Basics of Meditation

49

6.2 Techniques to Enhance Focus and Concentration

52

6.3 Mindfulness in Decision Making

54

Chapter 7: Managing Public Speaking Anxiety

58

7.1 Identifying Triggers and Symptoms

58

7.2 Yogic Strategies for Confidence Building

60

7.3 Pre-Speech Preparation and Post-Speech Recovery

63

Chapter 8: Cultivating Empathy and Patience in Governance

67

8.1 The Role of Compassion in Politics

67

8.2 Patience as a Strategic Asset

69

8.3 Empathy-Enhancing Practices

71

Chapter 9: Ethical Alignment and Good Governance

75

9.1 Exploring Yoga's Ethical Precepts

75

9.2 Aligning Personal Values with Public Service

78

9.3 Case Studies on Integrity, Transparency, and Accountability

81

Chapter 10: Creating a Culture of Wellness within Political Institutions

85

10.1 Benefits of Organizational Wellness Programs

85

10.2 Implementing Yoga Initiatives in Governmental Bodies

88

10.3 Measuring Impact on Team Cohesion and Productivity

91

Chapter 11: Overcoming Challenges to Consistent Practice

95

11.1 Identifying Common Obstacles

95

11.2 Strategies for Maintaining Regularity

97

11.3 Leveraging Community Support

99

Chapter 12: Short Yoga Breaks for Busy Schedules

104

12.1 Quick Practices for Office Settings

104

12.2 Incorporating Mindfulness Moments throughout the Day

106

12.3 Tips on Time Management

109

Chapter 13: Advanced Techniques for Seasoned Practitioners

113

13.1 Deepening Your Practice with Advanced Asanas

113

13.2 Exploring Higher States through Meditation

116

13.3 Engaging with the Global Yoga Community

119

Chapter 14: Navigating Complex Negotiations with Clarity

123

14.1 Applying Mindfulness to Communication

123

14.2 Strategies for Remaining Calm under Pressure

125

14.3 Building Consensus through Compassionate Dialogue

128

Chapter 15: Leading with Wisdom and Compassion

131

15.1 Lessons from Historical Leaders

131

15.2 Cultivating Self-Awareness

133

15.3 Integrating Wisdom into Decision-Making

135

Chapter 16: Ethical Leadership in Times of Crisis

139

16.1 Responding to Crisis with Mindfulness

139

16.2 Maintaining Integrity in Turbulent Times

141

16.3 Leading with Empathy and Compassion

143

Chapter 17: Towards a Future of Sustainable Leadership

147

17.1 Envisioning a New Era of Governance

147

17.2 Integrating Yoga into Political Culture

150

17.3 Creating a Legacy of Wisdom and Compassion

153

1

Introduction to Yoga for Politicians

1.1 The Need for Balance in Political Life

The realm of politics is inherently demanding, characterized by its high-pressure environment, constant public scrutiny, and the perpetual balancing act between personal convictions and public responsibilities. In this context, the pursuit of balance is not merely beneficial but essential for effective leadership and personal well-being. The integration of yoga into a politician's life offers a multifaceted solution to these challenges, providing tools for stress management, enhanced decision-making, and physical health.

At its core, the practice of yoga transcends physical exercise, encompassing mental and emotional disciplines that foster a state of equilibrium. For politicians, whose decisions can have far-reaching consequences, the clarity of mind and emotional stability nurtured through yoga are invaluable assets. Moreover, the emphasis on mindfulnessâ€"a cornerstone of yogic philosophyâ€"encourages a heightened awareness of the present moment. This can be particularly beneficial in navigating the complex dynamics of political negotiations and public engagements with a calm and focused demeanor.

In addition to these individual benefits, incorporating yoga into daily routines fosters a holistic sense of well-being that can ripple outwards, influencing one's interactions with colleagues, constituents, and even adversaries in more positive ways. By embodying the principles of balance, patience, and compassion learned on the mat, politicians can lead by exampleâ€"promoting a culture of civility and respect within the often divisive arena of politics.

- Stress Reduction: Yoga's breathing techniques and meditative practices are proven stress relievers that can help mitigate the chronic stress often experienced in political life.

- Improved Decision-Making: By promoting mental clarity and reducing impulsivity, yoga can enhance a politician's ability to make thoughtful decisions under pressure.

- Physical Stamina: The physical postures (asanas) improve flexibility, strength, and endurance—qualities that are essential for meeting the rigorous demands of political schedules.

- Emotional Resilience: Regular yoga practice cultivates an inner strength that aids politicians in facing criticism and adversity with grace and equanimity.

In conclusion, as political landscapes become increasingly complex and contentious, the ancient wisdom of yoga offers timely insights for modern leaders. Embracing yoga as both a personal practice and a professional tool can empower politicians to navigate their roles with greater effectiveness and integrity. Ultimately, by fostering balance in their own lives, they are better equipped to contribute to the balance needed in their communities and beyond.

1.2 Overview of Yoga's Benefits for Leaders

The integration of yoga into the lifestyle of political leaders and decision-makers transcends mere physical well-being, embedding itself as a cornerstone for mental clarity, emotional resilience, and enhanced leadership capabilities. The multifaceted benefits of yoga offer a holistic approach to navigating the complexities and pressures inherent in leadership roles.

At the heart of yoga's appeal to leaders is its profound impact on stress reduction. The high-stakes environment of politics, characterized by relentless scrutiny and the weight of decision-making, can lead to chronic stress and burnout. Yoga's breathing techniques (Pranayama) and meditative practices serve as powerful tools for managing stress, promoting a sense of calmness and focus that is crucial for effective leadership.

- Stress Reduction: Through deep breathing exercises and meditation, yoga helps in significantly lowering stress levels, enabling leaders to approach their duties with a clear mind.

- Improved Decision-Making: Yoga enhances cognitive functions, leading to better decision-making abilities. A calm mind fosters clarity and prevents impulsive reactions, allowing for thoughtful consideration of all aspects before making important decisions.

- Physical Stamina: Regular practice of yoga asanas strengthens the body's core, improves flexibility, and boosts overall stamina. This physical resilience is essential for leaders who often endure demanding schedules.

- Emotional Resilience: Yoga cultivates an inner strength that empowers leaders to handle criticism, setbacks, and adversity with grace. It encourages a perspective shift towards viewing challenges as opportunities for growth.

Beyond these individual benefits, yoga influences leadership styles by encouraging qualities such as empathy, patience, and compassion. These attributes are invaluable in fostering positive relationships within teams, between colleagues, and across constituencies. Leaders who practice yoga often report improved communication skills and a greater ability to inspire and motivate those around them.

Incorporating yoga into daily routines also promotes mindfulnessâ€"a heightened state of awareness that enables leaders to be fully present in the moment. This mindfulness can transform interactions with others by fostering active listening, empathy, and understanding from multiple perspectives.

In conclusion, the adoption of yoga by political leaders can significantly enhance their effectiveness by not only improving their personal health but also enriching their leadership qualities. As they embody balance and harmony through their own practices, they set a powerful example for others to followâ€"cultivating an environment where mutual respect and constructive dialogue flourish.

1.3 The Journey Ahead

The path to integrating yoga into the life of a political leader is both promising and challenging. It requires a commitment that goes beyond occasional practice, embedding itself into the very fabric of daily routines and decision-making processes. This journey ahead for politicians who choose to embrace yoga is not just about personal transformation but also about redefining leadership in the modern world.

Embarking on this journey begins with understanding that yoga is more than physical exercise; it's a comprehensive system that encompasses mental, emotional, and spiritual well-being. For politicians, this means adopting practices that foster inner peace and resilience, enabling them to navigate the turbulent waters of public service with grace and steadfastness.

- Personal Transformation: Politicians will experience a profound personal transformation through regular yoga practice. This transformation extends beyond physical health improvements to include enhanced mental clarity, emotional stability, and a deeper sense of purpose.

- Cultivating Mindfulness: Yoga encourages mindfulness, which can significantly alter how leaders perceive challenges and interact with others. A mindful politician is more likely to approach situations with empathy, patience, and an open mindâ€"qualities essential for constructive dialogue and effective governance.

- Leadership Redefined: By embodying the principles of yoga, politicians can inspire change within their communities and beyond. Leadership then becomes not just about guiding others but also about serving as a beacon of balance, integrity, and compassion.

The journey ahead also involves overcoming obstacles such as time constraints and societal misconceptions about yoga. Politicians must navigate these challenges with determination, recognizing that the benefits of their practice extend far beyond themselves. As they become more grounded in their yoga practice, they set a powerful example for others to follow—demonstrating that true leadership emanates from a place of inner strength and harmony.

In conclusion, the journey ahead for politicians practicing yoga is one of profound growth and opportunity. It offers a pathway to transform not only their own lives but also the very essence of political leadership in today's world. By committing to this path, leaders can forge a legacy of peace, resilience, and positive change—a testament to the transformative power of yoga.

References:

- Gardner, H. (2019). "Yoga and Leadership: A New Perspective on Organizational Success." Journal of Business Ethics.

- Kabat-Zinn, J. (2005). "Wherever You Go, There You Are: Mindfulness Meditation in Everyday Life." Hyperion.

- Brown, K.W., & Ryan, R.M. (2003). "The Benefits of Being Present: Mindfulness and Its Role in Psychological Well-being." Journal of Personality and Social Psychology.

- Iyengar, B.K.S. (2005). "Light on Life: The Yoga Journey to Wholeness, Inner Peace, and Ultimate Freedom." Rodale Books.

2

Understanding Stress and Leadership

2.1 The Impact of Stress on Decision-Making

The intricate relationship between stress and decision-making is a critical area of exploration, particularly for individuals in leadership roles. Stress, an inevitable aspect of the high-stakes political arena, can significantly influence the cognitive processes underlying decision-making. Understanding this impact is essential for developing strategies to mitigate negative effects and enhance leadership effectiveness.

Stress triggers the body's fight or flight response, releasing hormones such as cortisol and adrenaline. While these hormonal changes prepare the body to respond to immediate threats, they can impair cognitive functions crucial for making well-considered decisions. High stress levels can lead to tunnel vision, limiting a leader's ability to assess all available options and potential outcomes. This narrowed perspective can result in decisions that are reactive rather than strategic.

Moreover, chronic stress can deplete cognitive resources over time, leading to decision fatigue. This condition diminishes a leader's capacity to weigh the pros and cons of different actions effectively, making them more susceptible to choosing options that require less cognitive effort but may not be in their best interest or that of their constituents.

To counteract these challenges, incorporating practices such as mindfulness meditation and yogaâ€"proven stress reducersâ€"can be beneficial. These practices enhance mental clarity and emotional regulation, enabling leaders to approach decision-making with a calm and focused mind. Additionally, fostering an environment that encourages regular breaks and supports work-life balance can help mitigate the adverse effects of stress on decision-making capabilities.

- Impaired Judgment: Under stress, leaders might rely heavily on heuristics or mental shortcuts, which can lead to biased or flawed decisions.

- Risk-Taking Behavior: Stress can alter risk perception, with some leaders becoming overly cautious while others take excessive risks without fully considering the consequences.

- Emotional Reactivity: Heightened stress levels increase emotional reactivity, which can cloud judgment and lead to decisions driven by emotion rather than rational analysis.

In conclusion, recognizing the profound impact of stress on decision-making is crucial for effective leadership. By adopting strategies aimed at managing stress levels, leaders can preserve their cognitive resources, maintain emotional equilibrium, and make decisions that are thoughtful, balanced, and aligned with their goals and values.

2.2 Leadership Challenges in the Political Arena

The political arena presents a unique set of challenges for leaders, significantly influenced by the inherent stress of their roles. These challenges are multifaceted, encompassing the need to make critical decisions under pressure, manage public perception, and navigate complex interpersonal dynamics within and outside their political parties. The ability to effectively address these issues is crucial for maintaining leadership effectiveness and achieving policy goals.

One of the primary challenges is decision-making under stress. Political leaders often face situations where they must make quick decisions with far-reaching consequences. The stress associated with these high-stakes decisions can impair judgment and lead to choices that are not fully considered. This environment demands strategies that enhance cognitive function and emotional regulation, enabling leaders to remain clear-headed and focused despite external pressures.

In conclusion, leadership in the political arena demands a robust set of skills to navigate its inherent challenges successfully. By understanding the impact of stress on decision-making processes and adopting strategies to manage it effectively, political leaders can enhance their capacity to lead with clarity, purpose, and resilience.

- Public Scrutiny: Leaders in the political sphere operate under intense observation, where every decision and action is subject to public scrutiny. This constant attention can amplify stress levels, making it challenging to maintain composure and confidence.

- Interpersonal Dynamics: Navigating relationships with other politicians, stakeholders, and constituents requires a delicate balance of assertiveness, diplomacy, and tact. Missteps in this area can have significant repercussions for a leader's agenda and public image.

- Policy Implementation: Translating vision into actionable policy involves overcoming bureaucratic hurdles, legislative opposition, and sometimes public resistance. Achieving meaningful progress often requires compromise and negotiation skills.

To mitigate these challenges, political leaders can benefit from developing resilience strategies that enable them to adapt to stressors while maintaining their effectiveness. Practices such as engaging in regular physical activity, seeking support from trusted advisors or mentors, and prioritizing mental health through mindfulness or relaxation techniques can be invaluable. Additionally, fostering an environment of open communication within their teams encourages collaboration and shared problem-solving, reducing the burden on individual leaders.

2.3 How Yoga Offers Solutions

In the context of leadership, particularly within the high-pressure environment of the political arena, yoga emerges as a potent tool for addressing and mitigating the multifaceted challenges leaders face. The practice of yoga transcends mere physical exercise, encompassing mental, emotional, and spiritual dimensions that collectively foster resilience, clarity, and enhanced decision-making capabilities.

The essence of yoga lies in its holistic approach to stress management and personal well-being. Through a combination of postures (asanas), breath control techniques (pranayama), and meditation (dhyana), yoga offers a comprehensive methodology for cultivating inner peace, focus, and emotional stability. These qualities are invaluable for leaders who must navigate the complexities of political dynamics under constant scrutiny.

- Enhanced Cognitive Function: Regular engagement in yoga has been shown to improve concentration, memory, and cognitive flexibility. For political leaders dealing with complex issues and requiring sharp mental acuity for decision-making, these benefits can significantly enhance their effectiveness.

- Emotional Regulation: Yoga's emphasis on mindfulness and present-moment awareness aids in managing emotions effectively. Leaders can better handle stress-induced reactions such as anger or frustration, enabling them to respond to challenging situations with composure.

- Physical Health: The physical aspects of yoga contribute to improved overall health, including increased energy levels and reduced symptoms of stress-related conditions. A healthy body supports a healthy mind, equipping leaders with the stamina required for their demanding roles.

- Spiritual Insight: Beyond tangible benefits, yoga offers pathways to deeper self-understanding and connection with universal values such as compassion and empathy. These insights can inspire more ethical leadership practices and foster a sense of connectedness with constituents.

Incorporating yoga into the routine of political leaders can thus serve as a powerful strategy not only for personal health but also for enhancing leadership quality. By promoting balance between mind, body, and spirit, yoga equips leaders with the tools needed to lead with integrity, vision, and an unwavering calm amidst the storms they may face.

In conclusion, as we explore solutions to the challenges highlighted in leadership within high-stress environments like politics, it becomes clear that practices like yoga offer more than just physical benefits; they provide a foundation for developing the inner resources necessary for effective leadership. Embracing such holistic approaches could be key in transforming how leaders navigate their rolesâ€"leading not just with their minds but from a place of holistic well-being.

References:

- Gard, T., Noggle, J.J., Park, C.L., Vago, D.R., & Wilson, A. (2014). Potential self-regulatory mechanisms of yoga for psychological health. Frontiers in Human Neuroscience, 8, 770.

- Gothe, N.P., Keswani, R.K., & McAuley, E. (2016). Yoga practice improves executive function by attenuating stress levels. Biological Psychology, 121(Part A), 109-116.

- Ross, A., & Thomas, S. (2010). The health benefits of yoga and exercise: a review of comparison studies. The Journal of Alternative and Complementary Medicine, 16(1), 3-12.

- Saunders, R., Frierson, G.M., & Mosby T.T. (2017). The role of yoga in relieving medical student anxiety and stress. Journal of Alternative and Complementary Medicine, 23(4), 258-263.

3

Foundations of Yoga Practice

3.1 History and Philosophy of Yoga

The history and philosophy of yoga are as rich and deep as the practice itself, tracing back over 5,000 years in ancient India. Yoga's journey from the East to becoming a global phenomenon speaks volumes about its universal appeal and adaptability. Its roots can be found in the Vedic tradition, where it was initially a meditative practice aimed at understanding the outer world by delving into the inner cosmos of the human experience. This spiritual endeavor was first documented in the Vedas, ancient Indian texts that are among the oldest sacred scriptures in Hinduism.

Yoga's philosophical underpinnings are further explored in the Upanishads, a collection of texts that emphasize the importance of detaching from ego and material desires to achieve ultimate reality or

Brahman. The Bhagavad Gita, another seminal text, introduces yoga as a multifaceted path to spiritual growth, including devotion (Bhakti), knowledge (Jnana), and disciplined action (Karma). However, it is in Patanjali's Yoga Sutras, compiled around 400 CE, that yoga's philosophy is systematically outlined. Patanjali describes an eight-fold path (Ashtanga) to enlightenment, which includes ethical standards (Yamas), self-discipline (Niyamas), posture (Asana), breath control (Pranayama), sensory withdrawal (Pratyahara), concentration (Dharana), meditation (Dhyana), and ultimately absorption into the divine (Samadhi).

The evolution of yoga did not stop with these ancient texts; it continued to grow and spread across continents and cultures. In the late 19th and early 20th centuries, yoga masters began to travel to the West, bringing with them their knowledge and practices. This period marked a significant shift as yoga started being incorporated into physical fitness programs, leading to what some refer to as Modern Postural Yoga. Despite this shift towards physicality, many practitioners today still seek out yoga for its spiritual benefits and its potential for personal transformation.

- The Vedas: Highlighting yoga's origins within Vedic traditions.

- The Upanishads: Emphasizing detachment for spiritual growth.

- The Bhagavad Gita: Introducing different paths of yoga.

- Patanjali’s Yoga Sutras: Outlining an eight-fold path to enlightenment.

- Modern Postural Yoga: The adaptation of yoga into physical fitness regimes worldwide.

In conclusion, understanding the history and philosophy of yoga provides invaluable insights into its practices today. From its ancient roots as a means for spiritual inquiry and self-realization to its modern adaptations focusing on physical health and well-being, yoga remains a versatile tool for navigating life's challenges. Its enduring relevance speaks to humanity's ongoing quest for meaning beyond material success—a testament to yoga's profound impact on individuals across time and cultures.

3.2 Key Principles and Ethics of Yoga

The principles and ethics of yoga form the bedrock upon which the practice stands, guiding practitioners not just on the mat but in every aspect of life. Rooted in ancient wisdom, these ethical guidelines are as relevant today as they were thousands of years ago, offering a compass for navigating the complexities of modern living with integrity and compassion.

At the heart of yoga's ethical framework are the Yamas and Niyamas, often considered the first two limbs of Patanjali's Ashtanga Yoga. These tenets serve as moral imperatives to help cultivate a life of purpose, honesty, and respect for all living beings.

The Niyamas encourage personal observances that nurture self-discipline and inner strength:

- Ahimsa (Non-violence): This principle advocates for non-harm towards others and oneself. In contemporary context, it extends beyond physical harm to include words and thoughts, encouraging actions that promote peace and harmony.

- Satya (Truthfulness): Satya urges practitioners to live and speak their truth with kindness. It emphasizes the importance of honest communication that does not injure others.

- Asteya (Non-stealing): Beyond the literal interpretation of not taking what is not given, Asteya also encompasses respecting others' time, energy, and resources.

- Brahmacharya (Right use of energy): Traditionally associated with celibacy, Brahmacharya is now more broadly interpreted as using one's energy wisely â€" directing it towards personal growth and spiritual development rather than wasteful pursuits.

- Aparigraha (Non-greed): This principle teaches contentment with what one has, avoiding unnecessary accumulation of material possessions and fostering a sense of generosity.

- Saucha (Purity): Saucha refers to cleanliness of body, mind, and environment, inspiring practices that promote physical health and mental clarity.

- Santosha (Contentment): Encouraging acceptance and gratitude for what one has in the present moment, Santosha cultivates joy independent of external circumstances.

- Tapas (Discipline or Austerity): Tapas involves self-discipline practices that refine oneâ€™s character through challenges that foster resilience and commitment to oneâ€™s path.

- Svadhyaya (Self-study): This principle invites continuous learning about oneself through reflection on personal behaviors and study of yogic texts to deepen understanding.

- Ishvara Pranidhana (Surrender to a higher power): Ishvara Pranidhana encourages surrendering egoistic desires in favor of recognizing a force greater than oneself â€" fostering humility and devotion.

Incorporating these ethical practices into daily life enriches the yoga journey beyond physical postures by weaving spirituality into everyday actions. They guide individuals toward leading lives marked by compassion, integrity, discipline, humility â€" qualities that resonate deeply within society's fabric. By embodying these principles off the mat as well as on it; yogis contribute positively to their communities; creating ripples that can inspire collective shifts towards more mindful living globally. Thus; understanding; embracing;

practicing these key principles ethics lies at core transformative power yoga offers both individually collectively.

3.3 Establishing a Personal Practice

Establishing a personal yoga practice is a journey that moves beyond the physical postures to embrace the core principles and ethics of yoga, as outlined in the previous section. This process involves creating a dedicated space for practice, setting realistic goals, and cultivating discipline and consistency. By integrating the Yamas and Niyamas into this personal endeavor, practitioners can develop a holistic approach that nurtures both body and spirit.

The first step in establishing a personal practice is identifying what motivates you. Whether seeking physical health, mental clarity, emotional balance, or spiritual growth, understanding your intentions sets the foundation for your journey. This clarity helps in tailoring your practice to meet your specific needs and aspirations.

- Creating a Dedicated Space: Designate a quiet, comfortable area in your home where you can practice undisturbed. This space should be inviting and filled with positive energy, encouraging you to return daily.

- Setting Realistic Goals: Start with achievable objectives that align with your current physical condition, lifestyle, and commitments. Gradually increase the complexity and duration of your practice as you progress.

- Cultivating Discipline: Consistency is key in deepening your yoga practice. Try to establish a routine by practicing at the same time each day. Remember that discipline also means listening to your body and allowing rest when needed.

Incorporating the Yamas and Niyamas into your personal practice enriches it by bringing mindfulness into how you live off the mat. For instance, practicing Ahimsa (non-violence) can guide you to be gentle with yourself during challenging poses or when facing limitations. Similarly, Santosha (contentment) encourages acceptance of where you are in your journey without comparing yourself to others.

To further support your personal practice, seek out resources such as books, online classes, or workshops that resonate with your goals. Engaging with the broader yoga community can provide inspiration and new insights into your own path.

In conclusion, establishing a personal yoga practice is an evolving process that reflects individual growth and understanding. By integrating the ethical principles of yoga into this personal endeavor, practitioners embark on a transformative journey that extends far beyond physical achievementsâ€"cultivating peace, balance, and fulfillment in all aspects of life.

References:

- Desikachar, T.K.V. "The Heart of Yoga: Developing a Personal Practice." This book offers a comprehensive guide to understanding and applying the principles of yoga in daily life.

- Iyengar, B.K.S. "Light on Yoga." A seminal text that provides detailed descriptions of postures and breathing techniques, helping practitioners deepen their physical practice.

- Farhi, Donna. "Bringing Yoga to Life: The Everyday Practice of Enlightened Living." Farhi explores how yoga's principles can be woven into the fabric of our daily existence for greater spiritual growth and well-being.

- McGonigal, Kelly. "Yoga for Pain Relief." This resource focuses on using yoga to manage pain and improve overall health, emphasizing mindfulness and self-compassion.

- Gates, Rolf. "Meditations from the Mat: Daily Reflections on the Path of Yoga." Gates offers insights into how the practice of yoga extends beyond the mat into every aspect of life.

4

Yoga Poses for Physical Stamina and Health

4.1 Essential Poses for Energy and Strength

The practice of yoga offers a myriad of benefits, not least among them the enhancement of physical stamina and energy levels. For individuals in demanding roles, such as those in the political sphere, cultivating these qualities is essential. This section delves into specific yoga poses that are particularly effective in building energy and strength, thereby supporting both the physical demands of leadership and the mental resilience required to navigate the complexities of governance.

Yoga, with its holistic approach to well-being, provides a powerful toolset for enhancing physical health and vitality. The poses described here have been selected for their efficacy in increasing core strength, improving flexibility, and boosting overall energy levels. Incorporating these poses into a regular practice can help mitigate the effects of stress, enhance decision-making capabilities, and foster a sense of groundedness amidst the chaos often encountered in political life.

Incorporating these poses into a daily routine can significantly impact one's physical stamina and energy levels. For politicians or anyone engaged in high-stress professions, these practices offer a pathway to maintaining not just physical health but also emotional resilience. By starting with even a few minutes each day dedicated to these poses can lead to profound changes over timeâ€"enhancing one's capacity for leadership by fostering a strong foundation of physical health from which to draw strength.

- Tadasana (Mountain Pose): This foundational pose helps improve posture, strengthens thighs, knees, and ankles while also helping to increase awareness and steadiness.

- Adho Mukha Svanasana (Downward-Facing Dog): A pivotal pose for strengthening the arms and legs while stretching the shoulders, hamstrings, calves, arches, and hands. It also energizes the body.

- Virabhadrasana (Warrior Pose): This series of poses not only builds focus and power but also invigorates the body by improving balance and stability.

- Bhujangasana (Cobra Pose): By opening up the chest and strengthening the spine, this pose facilitates deeper breathing which increases oxygen flow to boost energy levels.

- Dhanurasana (Bow Pose): This pose enhances flexibility in the back while simultaneously strengthening it; it also helps open up shoulder muscles and adds an energetic boost.

Moreover, beyond individual practice lies an opportunity for leaders to advocate for wellness within their organizations by integrating mindfulness practices like yoga into team routines or offering resources for staff members. Such initiatives not only contribute to individual well-being but can enhance team cohesion and productivity by reducing burnout rates among staff membersâ€”a testament to yoga's comprehensive benefits on both personal and professional levels.

4.2 Poses for Flexibility and Endurance

Building on the foundation of enhancing energy and strength, the journey into yoga continues with a focus on flexibility and endurance. These qualities are not only vital for physical health but also contribute significantly to mental resilience and emotional well-being. The practice of specific yoga poses aimed at increasing flexibility can lead to improved range of motion, reduced risk of injury, and enhanced blood flow. Meanwhile, poses that build endurance help in sustaining energy levels through long periods of physical or mental exertion, making them particularly beneficial for individuals facing the relentless demands of daily life.

The interplay between flexibility and endurance within a yoga practice can be seen as complementary forces. Flexibility allows for deeper engagement in poses, which in turn can enhance stamina by requiring the body to maintain postural integrity over time. This section explores several key poses that embody this synergy, offering a pathway to cultivate these essential attributes.

- Uttanasana (Standing Forward Bend): This pose stretches the hamstrings, calves, and hips while calming the mind and relieving stress. It challenges endurance as one aims to hold the pose comfortably over time.

- Paschimottanasana (Seated Forward Bend): Ideal for improving flexibility in the spine and legs, this forward bend also encourages patience and persistence as practitioners work gradually towards deepening their fold.

- Garudasana (Eagle Pose): By twisting limbs into a unique position, Eagle Pose tests balance while stretching the shoulders and hips. Holding this pose builds endurance in the legs and core muscles.

- Anjaneyasana (Low Lunge): An excellent pose for opening up the hip flexors and quads which enhances flexibility; practicing Anjaneyasana also builds endurance when maintained for multiple breaths.

- Setu Bandhasana (Bridge Pose): This backbend strengthens back muscles while opening chest and shoulders. It's beneficial for spinal flexibility and building muscular endurance in the glutes and hamstrings.

Incorporating these poses into regular practice not only advances one's physical capabilities but also fosters a deeper connection between mind, body, and spirit. As flexibility increases, so does one's ability to face life's challenges with grace; similarly, as endurance is built up, so too is one's capacity to persevere through adversity without losing heart. Thus, through dedicated practice of these selected yoga poses, individuals can achieve a harmonious balance that supports both their physical journeys and their broader life paths.

Beyond individual benefits, embracing these practices within community settings or organizational cultures promotes collective well-being. Encouraging participation in yoga sessions focused on flexibility and endurance can lead to healthier work environments where stress is managed more effectively, creativity flourishes due to increased mental clarity, and overall productivity is enhanced through improved physical health.

4.3 Recovery and Restorative Practices

The importance of recovery and restorative practices in yoga cannot be overstated, especially when considering the rigorous demands placed on the body through poses aimed at enhancing flexibility and endurance. While building strength and stamina is crucial, allowing the body time to recover and heal is equally vital. This section delves into the restorative side of yoga, which focuses on poses and practices designed to promote healing, reduce stress, and enhance overall well-being.

Restorative yoga practices are characterized by their gentle nature, utilizing props such as bolsters, blankets, and blocks to support the body in positions of comfort and ease. This approach facilitates deep relaxation without exerting effort in holding the pose. By engaging in these practices, individuals can experience profound benefits including improved circulation, a decrease in blood pressure, enhanced immune function, and a reduction in anxiety levels.

Ultimately, recovery and restorative yoga offer powerful tools for managing stress, healing from injuries, improving sleep patterns, and enhancing overall quality of life. They remind us that taking time to care for ourselves is not an indulgence but a necessary aspect of maintaining health and vitality.

- Supta Baddha Konasana (Reclining Bound Angle Pose): This pose helps open up the hips and chest, promoting relaxation throughout the body. Supported by cushions or bolsters under each knee, it allows for a gentle stretch without strain.

- Viparita Karani (Legs-Up-The-Wall Pose): Known for its ability to alleviate lower back pain and reduce leg swelling, this inversion offers relief after long periods of standing or sitting. It's also reputed to calm the nervous system.

- Balasana (Child's Pose): A fundamental restorative posture that soothes the nervous system and relieves stress by encouraging a state of relaxation while gently stretching the back muscles.

- Savasana (Corpse Pose): Often used as a final relaxation pose, Savasana allows for complete physical rest and mental release. It's essential for integrating the benefits of a yoga practice into both body and mind.

Incorporating these recovery and restorative practices into oneâ€™s routine creates a balanced approach to physical activity. It acknowledges the need for periods of active engagement as well as passive relaxationâ€"both of which are crucial for achieving optimal health. Moreover, these practices underscore the principle that sometimes less is more; by doing less physically demanding work but with greater mindfulness and intentionality, we can achieve profound effects on our health that rival those obtained through more vigorous exercise regimes.

References:

- Clark, M. (2015). "Restorative Yoga for Life: A Relaxing Way to De-stress, Re-energize, and Find Balance". This book provides a comprehensive guide to restorative yoga practices, emphasizing the importance of recovery and relaxation in a yoga routine.

- Krucoff, C., & Krucoff, M. (2000). "Healing Moves: How to Cure, Relieve, and Prevent Common Ailments with Exercise". The authors discuss various therapeutic exercises including restorative yoga poses that aid in healing and wellness.

- Lasater, J. H. (1995). "Relax and Renew: Restful Yoga for Stressful Times". Judith Hanson Lasater offers detailed instructions on restorative yoga poses that help reduce stress and rejuvenate the body and mind.

- Norberg, U., & Lundberg, A. (2009). "Yoga for Stress Relief: A Simple and Unique Three-Month Program for De-Stressing and Stress Prevention". This book includes sections on restorative yoga as part of its comprehensive approach to managing stress through yoga.

5

Breathing Techniques for Emotional Resilience

5.1 Understanding Pranayama

Pranayama, a Sanskrit word meaning "extension of the prÄ□á¹‡a (breath or life force)" or "breath control," is a cornerstone practice within the broader system of yoga. It involves techniques designed to enhance and manipulate the breath, with the aim of influencing the flow of prana in the body to achieve higher states of awareness, emotional resilience, and physical health. This ancient practice holds particular relevance for individuals in high-stress professions, such as politics, where managing stress and maintaining emotional equilibrium are critical.

The significance of pranayama extends beyond mere relaxation or stress management. It is a sophisticated discipline that integrates physical health with mental well-being and spiritual growth. By learning to control the breath, practitioners can influence their physiological state, calming or energizing themselves as needed. This ability to regulate one's internal state is invaluable in environments where external pressures are intense and unpredictable.

- Pranayama techniques vary widely, ranging from simple exercises like deep abdominal breathing to more advanced practices such as Kapalabhati (Skull Shining Breath) and Anulom Vilom (Alternate Nostril Breathing).

- Each technique has specific benefits and applications, making pranayama a versatile tool for addressing various physical and psychological challenges.

- Regular practice of pranayama can improve respiratory function, increase oxygenation of the blood, reduce stress levels, enhance concentration, and support overall well-being.

Incorporating pranayama into daily routines can be particularly beneficial for politicians and leaders facing high levels of stress and responsibility. By fostering a sense of inner calm and clarity, these breathing techniques empower individuals to make decisions with greater composure and insight. Furthermore, pranayama practices promote mindfulnessâ€"a quality that enhances empathy, patience, and ethical decision-making in leadership roles.

In conclusion, understanding and practicing pranayama offers profound benefits for emotional resilience and mental clarityâ€"qualities essential for effective leadership in any field. As part of a comprehensive approach to wellness that includes physical postures (asanas), meditation, and ethical living principles (yamas and niyamas), pranayama equips individuals with tools to navigate life's challenges with grace and strength.

5.2 Breathing Exercises for Stress Management

Stress management is an essential skill in today's fast-paced world, where the demands of work, personal life, and societal pressures can lead to overwhelming stress and anxiety. Breathing exercises, derived from the ancient practice of pranayama, offer a practical and accessible tool to mitigate stress, enhance emotional resilience, and maintain mental clarity amidst chaos. This section delves into specific breathing techniques that can be employed to manage stress effectively.

Breathing exercises for stress management are grounded in the principle that breath control can influence our physiological state, helping to reduce the levels of stress hormones in the body, lower heart rate, and promote relaxation. These techniques range from simple methods suitable for beginners to more advanced practices that can be developed over time.

- Deep Abdominal Breathing: This technique involves deep, even breaths from the abdomen rather than shallow breaths from the upper chest. It increases oxygen supply to your brain and stimulates the parasympathetic nervous system, promoting a state of calmness.

- 4-7-8 Breathing: Also known as "Relaxing Breath," this technique involves breathing in for 4 seconds, holding the breath for 7 seconds, and exhaling slowly for 8 seconds. This pattern helps reduce anxiety by increasing awareness of breath and focusing the mind on a calming rhythm.

- Box Breathing: This method requires you to breathe in for a count of four, hold for four, exhale for four, and then hold again for four seconds. It is particularly useful in high-stress situations as it helps regulate the autonomic nervous system.

Incorporating these breathing exercises into daily routines does not require significant time commitments or special equipment; they can be practiced anywhereâ€"at home, at work during a break or even while commuting. Regular practice not only aids in immediate stress relief but also contributes to long-term health benefits such as improved respiratory efficiency and enhanced mental focus.

To maximize effectiveness, individuals should choose a quiet environment free from distractions where they can sit comfortably with their back straight. Closing the eyes may help increase concentration on breathing patterns and facilitate deeper relaxation. Starting with just a few minutes per day can make a significant difference in managing stress levels and enhancing overall well-being.

In conclusion, breathing exercises offer a powerful tool for managing stress by harnessing the intrinsic connection between mind and body through breath control. By integrating these practices into daily life, individuals can cultivate greater emotional resilience and navigate life's challenges with increased composure and clarity.

5.3 Integrating Breathwork into Daily Routines

Integrating breathwork into daily routines is a transformative strategy for enhancing emotional resilience and managing stress with agility. This practice, rooted in ancient traditions, has gained modern relevance as individuals seek accessible ways to navigate the complexities of contemporary life. By embedding breath control techniques into regular activities, one can create a sustainable habit that fosters mental clarity, emotional stability, and physiological well-being.

The integration of breathwork into daily life begins with recognizing moments throughout the day that lend themselves to brief periods of mindfulness and breathing exercises. These opportunities can range from structured settings to spontaneous intervals that arise amidst our daily tasks.

- Morning Rituals: Starting the day with a few minutes of deep abdominal breathing or the 4-7-8 technique can set a positive tone for the day ahead, enhancing focus and calmness.

- Work Breaks: Incorporating short breathing sessions during breaks at work can help mitigate stress, refocus the mind, and boost productivity. Even a few minutes can reset your mental state.

- Commute Times: For those who commute, using this time to practice controlled breathing (while ensuring safety) can transform potentially stressful or wasted time into rejuvenating intervals.

- Evening Wind-down: Ending the day with breath-focused practices aids in releasing accumulated stress and preparing the body for restorative sleep.

To effectively integrate these practices, it's beneficial to establish cues or reminders throughout your environment. Digital reminders on phones or computers, visual cues like sticky notes in strategic locations, or pairing breathwork with habitual activities (like drinking coffee) can reinforce this new habit. Consistency is key; therefore, starting small and gradually increasing the duration or frequency of practice will yield more sustainable results over time.

Beyond individual benefits, integrating breathwork into daily routines also has potential social implications. Sharing these practices within communities or through social networks can foster collective well-being and resilience. As individuals become more adept at managing their own stress and emotions through breath control, they are better equipped to support others around them.

In conclusion, making breathwork an integral part of daily routines is not just about combating stress; it's about embracing a lifestyle that prioritizes mental health and well-being. With regular practice, individuals can unlock profound benefits that ripple across all facets of lifeâ€"enhancing personal growth, improving relationships, and contributing to a healthier society.

References:

- Brown, R.P., & Gerbarg, P.L. (2005). Sudarshan Kriya Yogic breathing in the treatment of stress, anxiety, and depression: Part Iâ€"neurophysiologic model. Journal of Alternative and Complementary Medicine, 11(1), 189-201.

- Ma, X., Yue, Z.Q., Gong, Z.Q., Zhang, H., Duan, N.Y., Shi, Y.T., Wei, G.X., & Li, Y.F. (2017). The Effect of Diaphragmatic Breathing on Attention, Negative Affect and Stress in Healthy Adults. Frontiers in Psychology, 8:874.

- Nestor, J. (2020). Breath: The New Science of a Lost Art. Riverhead Books. This book explores the history and science behind breathing techniques and their impact on health.

- Perciavalle, V., Blandini, M., Fecarotta, P., Buscemi, A., Di Corrado D., Bertolo L., Fichera F., Coco M. (2017). The role of deep breathing on stress. Neurological Sciences : Official Journal of the Italian Neurological Society and of the Italian Society of Clinical Neurophysiology, 38(3), 451-458.

6

Meditation Practices for Mental Clarity

6.1 Basics of Meditation

The practice of meditation, while ancient in its origins, offers timeless benefits that are particularly relevant in the modern political sphere. At its core, meditation is a tool for cultivating mental clarity, emotional stability, and a heightened sense of awareness—all attributes that can significantly enhance the effectiveness of political leadership. This section delves into the foundational aspects of meditation, elucidating how these practices can be seamlessly integrated into the demanding lives of politicians to foster resilience and strategic thinking.

Meditation begins with understanding the importance of breath and posture. These initial steps lay the groundwork for deeper practices that lead to significant improvements in stress management and decision-making processes. By focusing on breathing techniques, individuals learn to control their physiological responses to stress, enabling them to remain calm and composed in high-pressure situations. Similarly, adopting specific postures during meditation not only enhances physical comfort but also promotes mental alertnessâ€"two essential components for enduring lengthy legislative sessions or engaging in complex negotiations.

- Introduction to Breathwork: Learning how controlled breathing can influence oneâ€™s emotional state and stress levels.

- Posture for Presence: Exploring how physical alignment can impact mental focus and clarity.

- Mindfulness Meditation: Developing an awareness of the present moment to reduce anxiety and improve concentration.

In addition to these practical techniques, this section emphasizes the value of consistency in meditation practice. Just as political skills are honed over time through experience and reflection, the benefits of meditation are most profound when the practice is regular and integrated into daily routines. Politicians who commit to a consistent meditation practice report enhanced abilities to navigate complex political landscapes with greater ease and insight.

Ultimately, by embracing the basics of meditation, political leaders can unlock new dimensions of their capabilities. This not only enriches their personal well-being but also equips them with the inner resources needed to serve with greater compassion, integrity, and effectiveness. As we continue exploring more advanced meditation practices in subsequent sections, it becomes clear that these foundational techniques are not just preliminary steps but are integral components of a holistic approach to leadership excellence.

6.2 Techniques to Enhance Focus and Concentration

In the realm of meditation, focus and concentration are not merely by-products but essential skills that can be developed through specific techniques. These practices are crucial for anyone looking to deepen their meditation experience or enhance their mental clarity in daily activities. By honing focus and concentration, individuals can achieve a greater sense of presence, reduce mind wandering, and improve cognitive functions.

The journey towards enhanced focus begins with the understanding that our attention is a trainable resource. Just as athletes build physical strength through targeted exercises, individuals can strengthen their mental focus using specialized meditation techniques. These methods are designed to cultivate a single-pointed concentration, allowing practitioners to direct their attention more effectively and sustain it for longer periods.

- Mindfulness of Breathing: This foundational technique involves focusing on the breath as it enters and exits the body. Practitioners learn to observe the breath without attempting to control it, which helps in anchoring the mind in the present moment and reducing distractions.

- Concentration Mantras: The use of mantras, or repeated phrases, can serve as a focal point for concentration. By silently repeating a mantra, individuals can keep their thoughts centered and minimize external distractions.

- Visualization Practices: Engaging the mind's eye through visualization can significantly boost concentration levels. Whether itâ€™s picturing a serene landscape or visualizing an object with great detail, this technique helps in focusing mental resources on a single point of interest.

Beyond these techniques, creating an environment conducive to focus is equally important. A quiet space free from interruptions allows practitioners to delve deeper into their meditation without being pulled away by external stimuli. Additionally, setting aside dedicated time for practice reinforces the importance of these exercises in oneâ€™s routine, further supporting the development of concentration skills.

Ultimately, enhancing focus and concentration through meditation is not just about achieving better meditative states; it's about enriching all facets of life by fostering a sharper mind and a heightened sense of awareness. As individuals become more adept at controlling where they direct their attention, they unlock new levels of productivity, creativity, and emotional balanceâ€"qualities that are invaluable in both personal growth and professional success.

6.3 Mindfulness in Decision Making

Mindfulness, a practice deeply rooted in meditation, extends its benefits far beyond the cushion, influencing various aspects of daily life including decision-making processes. Embracing mindfulness in decision making transforms how choices are approached, leading to outcomes that are not only thoughtful but also aligned with one's deeper values and goals. This section delves into the pivotal role mindfulness plays in enhancing the quality of decisions made in both personal and professional contexts.

At its core, mindfulness involves maintaining a moment-by-moment awareness of our thoughts, feelings, bodily sensations, and surrounding environment with openness and curiosity. When applied to decision making, it equips individuals with the ability to observe their options and potential outcomes without immediate judgment or emotional reactivity. This pause creates a space for clarity and discernment, allowing for more informed and considered decisions.

Beyond individual benefits, mindful decision making fosters a culture of empathy and understanding within teams and organizations. By considering diverse perspectives mindfully before arriving at a conclusion, leaders can make inclusive decisions that reflect collective interests rather than personal biases.

- Reducing Impulsivity: Mindfulness curtails the tendency to make hasty decisions based on immediate emotions or biases. By fostering an attitude of patience, it encourages individuals to weigh their options carefully and consider long-term consequences rather than succumbing to impulsive choices.

- Enhancing Emotional Intelligence: Mindful decision making enhances emotional intelligence by promoting an understanding of one's emotional responses. Recognizing how emotions influence choices helps in navigating complex decisions with greater ease and confidence.

- Improving Focus: Just as meditation practices enhance focus and concentration, mindfulness sharpens mental clarity during the decision-making process. It aids in filtering out distractions and focusing on what truly matters, leading to more effective problem-solving strategies.

In essence, integrating mindfulness into decision-making processes does not merely improve the quality of decisions; it transforms the approach towards challenges into one marked by calmness, clarity, and compassion. Whether it's choosing between job offers or resolving interpersonal conflicts, mindfulness serves as a guiding light that illuminates paths previously obscured by confusion or haste. As such, cultivating a mindful approach to decisions is invaluable for anyone seeking to navigate life's complexities with grace and wisdom.

References:

- Kabat-Zinn, J. (1994). Wherever You Go, There You Are: Mindfulness Meditation in Everyday Life. Hyperion.

- Langer, E.J. (1989). Mindfulness. Da Capo Press.

- Gilbert, P., & Choden. (2013). Mindful Compassion: How the Science of Compassion Can Help You Understand Your Emotions, Live in the Present, and Connect Deeply with Others. New Harbinger Publications.

- Williams, M., & Penman, D. (2011). Mindfulness: An Eight-Week Plan for Finding Peace in a Frantic World. Rodale Books.

- Siegel, D.J. (2010). Mindsight: The New Science of Personal Transformation. Bantam.

7

Managing Public Speaking Anxiety

7.1 Identifying Triggers and Symptoms

The journey to managing public speaking anxiety begins with a crucial step: identifying its triggers and symptoms. This understanding is not only foundational but also transformative for individuals, especially politicians, who regularly face high-pressure speaking situations. Recognizing the specific factors that provoke anxiety and the physical or emotional responses they elicit can empower speakers to adopt targeted strategies for mitigation.

Anxiety triggers in public speaking often stem from a fear of negative judgment, failure, or previous traumatic experiences related to speaking engagements. For politicians, these triggers might be magnified by the high stakes of political discourse, where every word can be scrutinized, and the impact of their message can have far-reaching consequences. Additionally, external factors such as the size of the audience, the formality of the setting, or even personal issues unrelated to the speech itself can exacerbate feelings of nervousness.

Symptoms of public speaking anxiety manifest both physically and psychologically. Physically, individuals may experience shaking hands or voice, rapid heartbeat, sweating, dry mouth, or even nausea. These symptoms are often accompanied by psychological effects like panic attacks, loss of focus, negative self-talk, memory lapses, or an overwhelming urge to escape the situation. It's important to note that these symptoms can create a vicious cycle; for example, worrying about shaking can increase nervousness which in turn causes more shaking.

- Understanding one's own body language and reactions under stress

- Recognizing patterns in negative thinking related to public speaking

- Identifying past experiences that may influence current perceptions of public speaking

By identifying these triggers and symptoms early on, politicians and other individuals facing public speaking challenges can begin to work on specific yoga practices designed to address them directly. Techniques such as focused breathing exercises help manage physical symptoms like rapid heartbeat and sweating by calming the nervous system. Meanwhile mindfulness practices support cognitive restructuring efforts aimed at overcoming negative thought patterns associated with public speaking anxiety.

In conclusion, understanding one's unique triggers and symptoms forms a critical foundation for effectively managing public speaking anxiety. This insight enables individuals to tailor their approach using tools like yoga and mindfulness that align with their personal experiences and challenges in this area.

7.2 Yogic Strategies for Confidence Building

The practice of yoga offers a holistic approach to managing public speaking anxiety, focusing on both the mind and body to cultivate confidence and calmness. Unlike conventional methods that may address only the symptoms, yogic strategies aim at the root causes of anxiety, promoting long-term resilience and self-assurance. This section delves into specific yogic practices that can be instrumental in building confidence for public speakers.

At the core of these strategies is the principle of mindfulness, which encourages present-moment awareness with a non-judgmental attitude. Mindfulness practices help individuals recognize and accept their feelings of anxiety without being overwhelmed by them. This acceptance is crucial in reducing the power that fear holds over an individual's performance.

- Pranayama (Breathing Exercises): Controlled breathing exercises such as Ujjayi (Victorious Breath) or Anulom Vilom (Alternate Nostril Breathing) are powerful tools in managing physiological symptoms of anxiety like rapid heartbeat and sweating. By focusing on slow, deep breaths, speakers can calm their nervous system before and during their presentation, enhancing focus and presence.

- Asanas (Physical Postures): Certain yoga poses can instill a sense of strength and stability, which are essential for confidence. For instance, standing poses like Tadasana (Mountain Pose) or Virabhadrasana (Warrior Pose) encourage good posture and open chest positioning, which are associated with increased self-confidence and authority.

- Dhyana (Meditation): Regular meditation practice improves concentration, clarity of thought, and emotional regulation—all vital for effective public speaking. Meditation can also reduce negative self-talk by fostering a mindset of compassion towards oneself.

- Savasana (Relaxation Pose): Ending a yoga session with Savasana helps integrate the benefits of the practice by allowing the body to fully relax and absorb the peace and stillness achieved through yoga. This deep relaxation technique can significantly lower stress levels, leaving individuals feeling refreshed and mentally clear.

Incorporating these yogic strategies into one's routine not only prepares an individual physically but also mentally for public speaking engagements. By developing a regular practice, speakers can build an inner foundation of calmness and confidence that supports them in facing high-pressure situations with poise. Moreover, these practices contribute to overall well-being, making them beneficial beyond just improving public speaking abilities.

In conclusion, yogic strategies offer comprehensive tools for building confidence through mindful awareness, breath control, physical strength, mental focus, and relaxation. As individuals become more adept at employing these techniques, they will likely find their anxiety around public speaking diminishes significantlyâ€"transforming what was once a source of dread into an opportunity for personal growth and connection with their audience.

7.3 Pre-Speech Preparation and Post-Speech Recovery

Pre-speech preparation and post-speech recovery are critical phases in the cycle of public speaking that often go overlooked but play a significant role in managing anxiety and enhancing performance. While yogic strategies offer a holistic approach to building confidence, integrating specific pre-speech and post-speech routines can further empower speakers, enabling them to approach their engagements with greater calmness and assurance.

Pre-Speech Preparation: The period leading up to a speech is pivotal for setting the tone of your presentation. It involves not only reviewing your material but also preparing your mind and body for the task ahead. Engaging in mindfulness exercises can help anchor you in the present moment, reducing pre-performance jitters. Techniques such as visualization can also be beneficial; envisioning a successful speech can boost confidence levels and create a positive mindset.

- Practicing deep breathing exercises or Pranayama before taking the stage can regulate your heart rate and calm your nerves, making it easier to focus on delivering your message effectively.

- Physical warm-ups or gentle yoga poses can release tension from the body, especially in areas like the shoulders and neck that tend to stiffen under stress.

- Mental rehearsal goes beyond simply reviewing notes; it involves running through your speech mentally, visualizing the flow of words, and anticipating audience reactions.

Post-Speech Recovery: After delivering a speech, it's important to engage in activities that facilitate recovery from the adrenaline rush and emotional exertion public speaking entails. This phase is about acknowledging your efforts, reflecting on your experience, and rejuvenating yourself for future engagements.

- Taking time for Savasana or another relaxation pose helps integrate the experience by allowing the body to absorb the peace achieved during performance, counteracting residual stress.

- A reflective practice such as journaling can provide insights into what went well and areas for improvement, fostering growth as a speaker.

- Celebrating small victories is crucial; recognizing your courage for facing public speaking challenges reinforces self-confidence and motivates continued progress.

Incorporating these pre-speech preparation and post-speech recovery techniques ensures a comprehensive approach to managing public speaking anxiety. By focusing on both anticipation of and reflection upon public speaking experiences, individuals can cultivate resilience against anxiety over time. This holistic strategy not only enhances immediate performance but also contributes to long-term development as an effective communicator.

References:

- Dale Carnegie, "The Quick and Easy Way to Effective Speaking". This book provides foundational insights into public speaking, emphasizing the importance of preparation and recovery.

- Thich Nhat Hanh, "The Miracle of Mindfulness". An exploration of mindfulness techniques that can be applied to pre-speech preparation to calm nerves and focus the mind.

- B.K.S. Iyengar, "Light on Yoga". Offers detailed descriptions of yoga poses and breathing exercises beneficial for physical and mental preparation before speeches.

- James Clear, "Atomic Habits". While not specifically about public speaking, this book discusses habit formation that can include pre-speech routines and post-speech reflection practices.

- Nancy Duarte, "Resonate: Present Visual Stories that Transform Audiences". Provides insights into engaging storytelling in speeches and the importance of reflecting on each presentation for continuous improvement.

8

Cultivating Empathy and Patience in Governance

8.1 The Role of Compassion in Politics

The concept of compassion in politics is often overshadowed by the pursuit of power and influence. However, integrating compassion into political leadership can lead to more effective governance, fostering environments where empathy, understanding, and patience are not just valued but practiced. This approach challenges the traditional view of politics as a battlefield and instead promotes it as a space for collective problem-solving and shared humanity.

Compassion in politics involves recognizing the needs and suffering of constituents and taking action to alleviate such issues. It requires leaders to step into the shoes of those they serve, understanding their concerns not just from a policy standpoint but from a human perspective. This empathetic approach can bridge divides, build trust among communities, and create policies that reflect the real needs of society.

Moreover, compassionate leadership in politics can inspire positive change beyond the confines of legislative chambers. When politicians lead with empathy, they set an example for citizens, encouraging a more cooperative and less divisive public discourse. This shift can transform political engagement from one characterized by antagonism to one rooted in mutual respect and understanding.

- Enhancing decision-making processes through emotional intelligence

- Building stronger connections between elected officials and their constituents

- Promoting policies that prioritize welfare and social justice

Incorporating compassion into politics also means reevaluating how success is measured in governance. Rather than focusing solely on economic indicators or power dynamics, compassionate governance values progress in terms of community well-being, environmental sustainability, and social equity. This holistic view acknowledges that true leadership is about serving effectively and creating conditions where all members of society can thrive.

In conclusion, the role of compassion in politics is pivotal for cultivating governance models that are inclusive, equitable, and responsive to the needs of all citizens. By embracing empathy as a core value, political leaders can navigate complex challenges with greater wisdom and foster a culture of kindness that extends beyond political arenas into everyday life.

8.2 Patience as a Strategic Asset

In the realm of governance, patience is often undervalued, yet it holds transformative power as a strategic asset. This section delves into how patience contributes to more thoughtful decision-making, fosters long-term relationships, and ultimately strengthens the fabric of political leadership. Unlike the fast-paced demands for immediate results that dominate contemporary politics, embracing patience allows leaders to navigate complex challenges with foresight and wisdom.

Patience in governance is not about inaction or passivity; rather, it's a deliberate approach to understanding issues deeply before making decisions. It involves taking the time to listen to diverse perspectives, weighing alternatives carefully, and considering the long-term implications of policies. This methodical process enhances decision-making by ensuring that solutions are not just reactive but are sustainable and inclusive.

- Facilitating deeper understanding of complex issues

- Enabling comprehensive evaluation of policy impacts

- Promoting inclusivity and consensus-building in decision processes

Moreover, patience plays a critical role in building and maintaining trust between elected officials and their constituents. By demonstrating a willingness to listen and engage over time, leaders can forge stronger connections with communities. This trust is essential for effective governance as it underpins public support for policies and initiatives. Furthermore, patience aids in conflict resolution by allowing time for tensions to deplete and enabling dialogue that seeks common ground.

In addition to its internal benefits within the political sphere, patience also has external advantages in diplomacy and international relations. Patient diplomacy can lead to more durable agreements by ensuring all parties feel heard and respected throughout negotiations. It allows for the careful navigation of sensitive issues and the cultivation of long-term partnerships based on mutual respect.

In conclusion, redefining patience as a strategic asset in governance offers a pathway towards more thoughtful, inclusive, and effective leadership. By prioritizing depth over speed and relationships over quick wins, political leaders can achieve outcomes that are both impactful and enduring. Embracing patience thus emerges not only as an ethical choice but as a pragmatic strategy for navigating the complexities of modern governance.

8.3 Empathy-Enhancing Practices

The cultivation of empathy within the sphere of governance is not merely a moral imperative but a strategic necessity for effective leadership and policy-making. Empathy-enhancing practices are essential tools for leaders seeking to understand and address the complex, multifaceted needs of their constituents. By fostering an environment where empathy is actively practiced, leaders can break down barriers of misunderstanding and mistrust, paving the way for more inclusive, equitable, and sustainable solutions.

Empathy in governance involves more than just the capacity to understand others' feelings; it requires a genuine commitment to recognizing diverse perspectives and experiences. This commitment can be manifested through various practices designed to deepen leaders' connection with their communities and stakeholders.

- Active Listening Sessions: Organizing forums where citizens can voice their concerns directly to policymakers without fear of judgment or reprisal encourages open dialogue and builds mutual respect.

- Cultural Exchange Programs: Facilitating opportunities for leaders to immerse themselves in the cultural contexts of different community groups enhances understanding beyond surface-level interactions.

- Collaborative Policy Development: Engaging a broad spectrum of voices in the policy-making process ensures that diverse viewpoints are considered, leading to more comprehensive and acceptable outcomes.

Beyond these initiatives, empathy-enhancing practices also extend to how policies are communicated and implemented. Transparent communication that acknowledges different perspectives and explains decisions in terms that resonate with various stakeholders can significantly increase public trust in government institutions. Moreover, implementing policies with flexibility allows adjustments based on feedback from those affected, demonstrating responsiveness and care for citizens' well-being.

Incorporating empathy into governance does not imply compromising on decisiveness or leadership strength; rather, it enriches decision-making by ensuring it is grounded in a deep understanding of the people it affects. By adopting empathy-enhancing practices, leaders can navigate the complexities of modern governance with greater sensitivity and effectiveness, ultimately achieving outcomes that reflect the collective best interests of their communities.

In conclusion, empathy-enhancing practices offer a pathway towards more humane and impactful governance. Through deliberate efforts to understand and incorporate diverse perspectives, leaders can foster an environment where empathy informs every aspect of decision-making processes. This approach not only strengthens democratic institutions but also reaffirms the fundamental value of compassion in guiding public service.

References:

- Brown, BrenÃ©. "Dare to Lead: Brave Work. Tough Conversations. Whole Hearts." Random House, 2018.This book discusses the role of vulnerability and empathy in leadership.

- Goleman, Daniel. "Emotional Intelligence: Why It Can Matter More Than IQ." Bantam Books, 1995.Goleman's work highlights the importance of emotional intelligence, including empathy, in effective leadership.

- Zak, Paul J. "The Neuroscience of Trust: Management Behaviors That Foster Employee Engagement." Harvard Business Review, January-February 2017 issue. This article explores how trust and empathy in leadership can enhance organizational performance.

- Krznaric, Roman. "Empathy: Why It Matters, and How to Get It." TarcherPerigee, 2014.Krznaric offers insights into how empathy can be cultivated and its significance in various aspects of life, including governance.

9

Ethical Alignment and Good Governance

9.1 Exploring Yoga's Ethical Precepts

The ancient practice of yoga extends far beyond the physical postures and breathing techniques commonly associated with it. At its core, yoga encompasses a comprehensive ethical framework designed to guide individuals towards a life of integrity, compassion, and self-discipline. This framework is particularly relevant for politicians and leaders who navigate the complex moral landscapes of governance and public service. Exploring Yoga's Ethical Precepts offers a pathway to understanding how these ancient guidelines can foster an environment of good governance and ethical alignment in today's political sphere.

Yoga's ethical precepts are encapsulated in the Yamas and Niyamas, which serve as moral imperatives and personal observances respectively. The Yamas include principles such as Ahimsa (non-violence), Satya (truthfulness), Asteya (non-stealing), Brahmacharya (moderation), and Aparigraha (non-greed). These principles encourage leaders to act with integrity, honesty, and fairness in their dealings, promoting peace and justice within their communities. For instance, practicing Ahimsa can inspire politicians to resolve conflicts through dialogue rather than aggression, embodying a leadership style that prioritizes harmony over discord.

The Niyamas encourage personal growth and self-discipline through practices like Saucha (cleanliness), Santosha (contentment), Tapas (discipline), Svadhyaya (self-study), and Ishvara Pranidhana (surrender to a higher power). These observances support leaders in cultivating inner strength, resilience, and clarity of purpose. By embracing Tapas, for example, politicians can develop the perseverance needed to tackle challenging issues with unwavering dedication.

Incorporating these ethical precepts into daily life can significantly enhance a leader's effectiveness by fostering a sense of accountability, empathy, and mindfulness. Through mindful reflection on the Yamas and Niyamas, political figures can align their actions with values that promote the well-being of society as a whole. This alignment not only benefits individual leaders but also sets a powerful example for others to follow, potentially transforming the culture within political institutions.

Ultimately, exploring Yoga's Ethical Precepts provides valuable insights into how ancient wisdom can inform modern leadership practices. By integrating these principles into their lives, politicians have the opportunity to lead with greater authenticity and compassion—qualities that are indispensable for navigating the complexities of governance in today's world.

9.2 Aligning Personal Values with Public Service

The intersection of personal values and public service is a critical area for those in governance and leadership roles. This alignment is essential not only for the integrity and effectiveness of public servants but also for fostering trust and respect within the communities they serve. When personal values are in harmony with the objectives of public service, leaders can navigate complex decisions with clarity and conviction, ensuring that their actions consistently benefit the public good.

Personal values such as honesty, accountability, empathy, and respect are foundational to ethical leadership. These values guide leaders in making decisions that are not only legally sound but also morally justifiable. For instance, a leader who deeply values transparency will strive to ensure open communication within their administration and with the public, thereby enhancing accountability and trust.

However, aligning personal values with public service is not without challenges. Public servants often face situations where personal beliefs may conflict with professional responsibilities or the expectations of their constituents. In such cases, it is crucial for leaders to engage in self-reflection and seek guidance from ethical frameworks like those provided by Yogaâ€™s Yamas and Niyamas. These ancient precepts offer valuable insights into managing conflicts between personal convictions and the demands of governance.

- Honesty (Satya) encourages leaders to be truthful in their communications, fostering an environment where trust can flourish.

- Non-violence (Ahimsa) guides decision-making processes towards peaceful resolutions, promoting harmony within communities.

- Self-discipline (Tapas) empowers leaders to persevere against challenges while maintaining their ethical standards.

In conclusion, aligning personal values with public service is paramount for any leader wishing to govern ethically and effectively. Through mindful reflection on one's core beliefs and adherence to universal ethical principles like those found in Yoga's Yamas and Niyamas, political figures can navigate the complexities of modern governance while upholding the highest standards of integrity and compassion.

Incorporating these principles into daily practices enables leaders to align their personal values with their professional duties effectively. By doing so, they not only enhance their own moral integrity but also set a positive example for others within their organization or community. Ultimately, the alignment of personal values with public service contributes to a more ethical, transparent, and compassionate governance system that prioritizes the well-being of all citizens.

This alignment also has broader implications for societal well-being. When leaders act in accordance with both their personal ethics and the demands of public service, they contribute to building stronger institutions that are capable of addressing social issues more effectively. Moreover, this congruence between individual morals and professional actions inspires confidence among constituents, leading to greater civic engagement and cooperation between the government and its citizens.

9.3 Case Studies on Integrity, Transparency, and Accountability

The principles of integrity, transparency, and accountability are not just theoretical concepts but are vital for the effective governance and ethical leadership within any organization or government. This section delves into real-world case studies that exemplify how these principles can be applied in practice, highlighting both successes and challenges faced by leaders in their quest to uphold these values.

One notable example involves a city mayor who implemented an "open data" initiative to increase transparency. By making city data accessible to the public, including budget allocations, spending reports, and project statuses, the administration fostered a culture of accountability. This initiative not only improved public trust but also encouraged civic engagement, as citizens were now able to contribute insights and feedback on city projects directly.

Another case study focuses on a corporate leader who prioritized integrity within their company's operations. Faced with significant pressure to compromise ethical standards for short-term gains, this leader instead chose to reinforce the company's commitment to ethical practices by establishing a robust compliance program. This program included regular ethics training for employees, a clear whistleblower policy, and strict enforcement of compliance standards across all levels of the organization. As a result, the company not only avoided potential legal issues but also strengthened its reputation in the industry.

These case studies underscore that while challenges are inevitable when striving for integrity, transparency, and accountability in leadership roles, proactive measures can significantly mitigate risks while enhancing organizational effectiveness and public trust. Moreover, they highlight that ethical leadership is not merely about avoiding wrongdoing but actively promoting good governance practices that benefit all stakeholders involved.

- A government agency's struggle with corruption serves as a cautionary tale about the importance of accountability mechanisms. After allegations of misuse of funds emerged, an independent audit was conducted which led to significant reforms within the agency. These reforms included stricter oversight procedures and enhanced transparency measures such as public reporting on expenditures.

- In another instance, a non-profit organization demonstrated exceptional integrity by voluntarily disclosing mistakes made in financial reporting. By taking immediate corrective action and openly communicating with stakeholders about the steps taken to rectify the errors, the organization maintained donor trust despite initial setbacks.

- A school district's approach to integrating transparency into its decision-making processes illustrates how educational institutions can lead by example. Through regular public meetings and online access to meeting minutes and decision rationales, parents and community members felt more involved in the educational system.

References:

- "Open Data's Impact on Civic Engagement: An Exploration of the Chicago Open Data Portal." Journal of Public Administration, Research, and Theory.

- "Building a Culture of Integrity: Lessons from the Corporate Sector." Harvard Business Review.

- "The Role of Independent Audits in Curbing Corruption within Government Agencies." Public Administration Review.

- "Transparency, Mistakes, and Trust: How Nonprofits Can Benefit from Being Open." Nonprofit Quarterly.

- "Engaging Communities through Transparency in School District Operations." Educational Leadership.

10

Creating a Culture of Wellness within Political Institutions

1.1 Benefits of Organizational Wellness Programs

The integration of wellness programs within political institutions offers a multitude of benefits that extend beyond the individual to foster a healthier, more productive organizational environment. In the context of political entities, where the pressures and demands can significantly impact mental and physical health, these programs are not just beneficial; they are essential. The advantages of implementing such initiatives range from improved employee health and reduced healthcare costs to enhanced job satisfaction and morale.

At the forefront, wellness programs are designed to support and encourage a holistic approach to employees' mental and physical health. This is particularly crucial in politics, where stress levels are notoriously high. By offering resources such as stress management workshops, mindfulness training, and physical fitness classes, organizations can help mitigate the adverse effects of stress, leading to improved concentration, decision-making capabilities, and overall mental clarity among politicians and staff alike.

In addition to these direct benefits, organizational wellness programs in political settings can serve as a model for public policy on health promotion and preventive care strategies. By demonstrating the effectiveness of such initiatives within their own ranks, political institutions can lead by example, advocating for policies that support wellness in the broader community. Ultimately, these programs contribute not only to the well-being of individuals within political organizations but also promote a culture of health that extends its influence far beyond office walls.

- Reduction in healthcare costs: Healthy employees tend to incur lower medical expenses, which translates into cost savings for the organization.

- Enhanced productivity: Wellness programs can lead to increased energy levels and reduced absenteeism due to illness or burnout, thereby boosting productivity.

- Improved job satisfaction: When institutions invest in the well-being of their staff, it fosters a sense of being valued and appreciated, enhancing job satisfaction and loyalty.

- Better team cohesion: Group activities related to wellness can improve interpersonal relationships among team members, fostering a more collaborative work environment.

In conclusion, incorporating wellness programs into political institutions presents an opportunity to address some of the unique challenges faced by those in governance while setting a precedent for prioritizing health at all levels of society. The benefits are clear: healthier individuals lead to stronger teams and more resilient leadership capable of navigating the complexities of today's political landscape with wisdom and compassion.

10.2 Implementing Yoga Initiatives in Governmental Bodies

The introduction of yoga initiatives within governmental bodies represents a transformative approach to enhancing the well-being and productivity of individuals operating within high-stress political environments. This strategy not only aligns with the broader objectives of organizational wellness programs but also introduces a unique set of benefits attributed to the practice of yoga itself. By integrating yoga into the daily routines of government employees, institutions can foster a culture of mindfulness, resilience, and physical health that transcends the personal benefits to positively impact the collective work environment.

Yoga, as a holistic discipline, offers more than just physical exercise; it is a comprehensive practice that combines physical postures, breath control, and meditation to improve overall health. The adaptability of yoga makes it an ideal component of wellness programs in governmental settings, where stress levels are high and the nature of work often demands prolonged periods of mental concentration. Regular yoga sessions can help alleviate stress, enhance mental clarity, and promote a sense of peace among employees, contributing to improved decision-making processes and increased productivity.

- Stress Reduction: Yoga's emphasis on mindfulness and breathing techniques can significantly lower stress levels among government officials and staff.

- Physical Health Benefits: Regular practice improves flexibility, strength, and posture while also preventing job-related injuries such as carpal tunnel syndrome or back pain.

- Mental Clarity: The meditative aspects of yoga encourage mental clarity and focus, essential qualities for effective policy-making and administration.

- Enhanced Team Cohesion: Group yoga sessions provide an opportunity for team-building activities that strengthen interpersonal relationships within political offices.

Incorporating yoga initiatives requires thoughtful planning and commitment from leadership within governmental bodies. It involves setting aside dedicated time for sessions, creating suitable spaces for practice, and possibly engaging qualified instructors who can tailor programs to meet the specific needs of participants. Moreover, by promoting these initiatives publicly, government bodies can lead by example in advocating for healthier lifestyles within their communities.

The implementation of yoga initiatives represents an innovative step towards addressing the multifaceted challenges faced by individuals in political institutions. Beyond offering immediate benefits to employees' health and well-being, these programs have the potential to enhance organizational performance through improved morale and reduced healthcare costs. Ultimately, by fostering a culture that values wellness at all levels of operation, governmental bodies can achieve greater resilience against the pressures inherent in political workspaces while setting a precedent for national health promotion strategies.

10.3 Measuring Impact on Team Cohesion and Productivity

The introduction of wellness initiatives, particularly yoga, within political institutions has marked a significant shift towards promoting health and well-being among government employees. However, the success of such programs is contingent upon their measurable impact on team cohesion and productivity. This section delves into the methodologies and metrics used to evaluate these outcomes, providing insights into how wellness practices contribute to the overall effectiveness of political institutions.

Assessing the impact of yoga and similar wellness activities on team cohesion involves examining changes in workplace dynamics and interpersonal relationships. Surveys and feedback mechanisms are instrumental in gathering data on employees' perceptions of their work environment before and after the implementation of wellness programs. Key indicators include increased collaboration, improved communication, and a reduction in conflicts among team members. These qualitative measures offer valuable insights into the social fabric of the workplace, highlighting the role of wellness practices in fostering a supportive and harmonious organizational culture.

In terms of productivity, quantifiable metrics such as absenteeism rates, job performance scores, and project completion times serve as critical benchmarks. A decline in absenteeism may indicate enhanced physical health and mental well-being among employees, attributing to regular participation in yoga sessions. Similarly, improvements in job performance scores can reflect heightened mental clarity, concentration, and decision-making abilities—core benefits associated with mindfulness exercises embedded within yoga practices.

- Employee Engagement Surveys: Tools that measure changes in employee satisfaction, motivation, and engagement levels post-implementation of wellness initiatives.

- Health-Related Outcome Measures: Data on reduced healthcare claims or lower instances of stress-related illnesses among employees participating in yoga programs.

- Performance Metrics: Analysis of work output quality, efficiency improvements, and achievement rates against organizational goals.

To ensure a comprehensive evaluation, combining both qualitative feedback from employees with quantitative performance data offers a holistic view of how wellness initiatives like yoga influence team cohesion and productivity. Moreover, longitudinal studies extending beyond immediate post-implementation periods can provide deeper insights into long-term benefits and sustainability of such programs within political institutions. Ultimately, measuring these impacts not only validates the importance of integrating wellness into organizational culture but also guides future enhancements to maximize benefits for both individuals and teams alike.

References:

- Grover, S.L., & Furnham, A. (2016). Coaching as a developmental intervention in organisations: A systematic review of its effectiveness and the mechanisms underlying it. Personnel Review, 45(5), 980-1004.

- Kerr, R., McHugh, M., & McCrory, M. (2009). HSE Management Standards and stress-related work outcomes. Occupational Medicine, 59(8), 574-579.

- Nielsen, K., Randall, R., Holten, A.-L., & GonzÃ¡lez, E.R. (2010). Conducting organizational-level occupational health interventions: What works? Work & Stress, 24(3), 234-259.

- Schaufenbuel, K. (2014). Why companies should invest in the mental health of employees. Forbes. Retrieved from https://www.forbes.com/

- Weston, D., Chandola, T., & WHO Healthy Workplace Framework and Model: Background and Supporting Literature and Practices. (2012). World Health Organization. Retrieved from http://www.who.int/

11

Overcoming Challenges to Consistent Practice

1.1 Identifying Common Obstacles

In the journey of integrating yoga into the demanding lives of politicians, identifying common obstacles is a crucial first step. This process not only acknowledges the unique challenges faced by political leaders but also sets the stage for developing tailored strategies to overcome these hurdles. The nature of political work, characterized by unpredictable schedules, high stress, and constant public scrutiny, presents distinct barriers to consistent yoga practice.

One significant obstacle is **time constraints**. Politicians often work long hours with little control over their schedules, making it difficult to find time for regular yoga sessions. Additionally, the **physical demands** of extensive travel and sitting through lengthy meetings can lead to fatigue and physical discomfort, which may deter individuals from engaging in physical activity.

Mental barriers also play a role. The high-pressure environment of politics can foster a mindset that views time spent on self-care as unproductive or selfish. There's also a cultural aspect within political circles that may undervalue or misunderstand the benefits of practices like yoga, seeing them as less critical than traditional forms of exercise or relaxation.

The **lack of tailored resources** specifically designed for political leaders is another hurdle. While there are countless yoga programs available, few address the unique needs and constraints of those in politics. This gap can make it challenging for politicians to find guidance that resonates with their experiences and offers practical solutions that fit into their hectic lives.

- Limited access to quiet spaces for practice within governmental buildings or while traveling.

- Skepticism or lack of support from peers and constituents who may not understand the value of yoga in enhancing leadership qualities.

- The challenge of maintaining privacy and security during practice sessions, especially for high-profile leaders.

To navigate these obstacles effectively, it's essential for political figures to recognize them openly and seek innovative solutions that honor both their personal well-being and professional responsibilities. By doing so, they pave the way toward a more balanced approach to leadership that incorporates mental clarity, emotional resilience, and physical staminaâ€"core benefits offered by consistent yoga practice.

11.2 Strategies for Maintaining Regularity

Maintaining regularity in any practice, especially for individuals with demanding careers such as politicians, requires strategic planning and commitment. The key to overcoming the common obstacles outlined previously lies in adopting a multifaceted approach that addresses time management, mental barriers, physical demands, and the need for tailored resources.

Here are several strategies designed to help maintain regularity in practices like yoga amidst the challenges of a political career.

Incorporating these strategies requires an initial investment of time and effort to establish new habits. However, once integrated into one's lifestyle, they not only facilitate regular practice but also contribute significantly to overall health and effectiveness in one's professional role. Overcoming the hurdles to consistent practice is not about finding more time but about making the most of available opportunities through smart planning and prioritization.

- Schedule Fixed Times for Practice: Just as important meetings are scheduled, so too should time for yoga practice. By setting aside fixed times each week, it becomes an integral part of the routine rather than an afterthought.

- Integrate Short Sessions: Recognizing that finding long periods may be challenging, integrating shorter sessions can make practice more manageable and less daunting. Even 15-20 minutes can be beneficial.

- Create a Dedicated Space: Having a dedicated space for practice can significantly enhance consistency. This doesn't need to be large; even a small, quiet corner that is always ready can reduce setup time and serve as a visual reminder.

- Leverage Technology: Utilizing online resources or apps designed for yoga can offer flexibility in terms of when and where practice occurs, making it easier to fit into unpredictable schedules.

- Engage with a Community: Being part of a community provides motivation and accountability. Whether it's joining a local class or an online group, connecting with others encourages regular participation.

- Set Realistic Goals: Setting achievable goals helps maintain focus and provides a sense of accomplishment that fuels further commitment.

- Prioritize Self-Care: Shifting the mindset to view self-care practices like yoga as essential rather than optional is crucial. Recognizing the benefits they bring to both personal well-being and professional performance can help justify their prioritization.

11.3 Leveraging Community Support

The importance of community support in maintaining a consistent practice cannot be overstated. While individual commitment plays a crucial role, the collective energy, motivation, and accountability found within a community offer unique benefits that significantly enhance the sustainability of any practice. This section delves into how leveraging community support can overcome common challenges to consistent practice, with a focus on strategies that harness the power of communal engagement.

Community support comes in various forms, from local groups and clubs to online forums and social media platforms. Each offers different advantages, but all share the common goal of fostering a supportive environment for members to share their experiences, challenges, and successes. Engaging with a community can transform practice from an isolated activity into a shared journey, making it more enjoyable and meaningful.

- Accountability Partners: Pairing up with someone or a small group within the community creates mutual accountability. Knowing that others are counting on your participation can be a powerful motivator to maintain regularity.

- Inspirational Stories: Hearing about how others have overcome obstacles can provide practical solutions and much-needed encouragement during difficult times. These stories often serve as reminders of what is possible with perseverance.

- Shared Resources: Communities often have access to resources that individuals may not know about or be able to afford on their own. From shared spaces for practice to group subscriptions for online classes or apps, pooling resources can make practice more accessible.

- Social Events: Organizing or participating in events such as workshops, retreats, or informal gatherings adds a social dimension to practice. These events can reinvigorate enthusiasm and deepen connections within the community.

Beyond these tangible benefits, being part of a community fosters a sense of belonging that is essential for long-term engagement. It provides an environment where individuals feel seen, heard, and valuedâ€"not just for their achievements but for their effort and dedication. This emotional support is particularly valuable during periods when motivation wanes or life circumstances change.

In conclusion, leveraging community support is not merely about attending events or being part of a group; it's about actively engaging with others who share similar goals and values. This engagement creates a symbiotic relationship where everyone contributes to and benefits from the collective strength of the community. By embracing this approach, individuals can significantly enhance their ability to maintain consistency in their practices amidst life's inevitable challenges.

References:

- Bandura, A. (1977). Social Learning Theory. Englewood Cliffs, NJ: Prentice Hall. This foundational text explores the impact of social environments on behavior, emphasizing the role of observational learning and social reinforcement.

- Deci, E.L., & Ryan, R.M. (2000). The "What" and "Why" of Goal Pursuits: Human Needs and the Self-

Determination of Behavior. Psychological Inquiry, 11(4), 227-268.This article discusses how community support can fulfill basic human needs for autonomy, competence, and relatedness, thereby enhancing motivation and engagement.

- Putnam, R.D. (2000). Bowling Alone: The Collapse and Revival of American Community. New York: Simon & Schuster. Putnam's book examines how social connections have diminished in modern society and suggests ways to rebuild these networks to foster communal support.

- Zakrzewski, V. (2013). The Science of a Happy Start-up Community. Greater Good Magazine. Retrieved from https://greatergood.berkeley.edu/article/item/the_scien ce_of_a_happy_start_up_community This online article provides insights into how happiness and success in start-up communities are influenced by practices that promote positive relationships and a sense of belonging.

12

Short Yoga Breaks for Busy Schedules

12.1 Quick Practices for Office Settings

In today's fast-paced work environment, finding time for extensive yoga sessions can be challenging, especially in office settings where stress levels are high and time is a premium. Recognizing this, quick yoga practices tailored for the office offer a practical solution. These short bursts of physical activity not only fit seamlessly into busy schedules but also provide immediate benefits such as stress relief, increased energy, and improved focus.

One of the key advantages of incorporating yoga into the office setting is its versatility. Yoga practices can range from simple desk-based stretches to more comprehensive sequences that require minimal space and no special equipment. This flexibility ensures that employees can engage in yoga without needing to change clothes or have access to a gym.

- Desk stretches target common tension areas like the neck, shoulders, and back. These can be performed while seated or standing next to your desk, making them ideal for short breaks between tasks.

- Breathing exercises, or pranayama, are another cornerstone of office yoga. Deep breathing techniques can be done quietly at one's desk to calm the mind and reduce stress levels instantly.

- Standing poses such as Mountain Pose (Tadasana) or Tree Pose (Vrikshasana) can be integrated into shorter breaks to improve balance and posture while stimulating circulation.

Ultimately, integrating quick yoga breaks into the workday is an effective strategy for managing stress and promoting well-being in office settings. By offering accessible ways to practice yoga at work, employees can maintain their physical health and mental clarity amidst their busy schedules.

In addition to physical postures and breathing exercises, mindfulness meditation offers a mental break from the demands of work. A brief meditation session can help clear the mind, enhance concentration, and boost productivity. Even just a few minutes spent in mindful observation or guided relaxation can make a significant difference in one’s day.

The implementation of quick yoga practices in office settings not only benefits individual employees by enhancing their well-being but also contributes positively to the overall workplace atmosphere. Reduced stress levels lead to better decision-making abilities and interpersonal relationships, fostering a more harmonious work environment. Moreover, these practices signal an employer’s commitment to supporting employee health and wellness, which can improve job satisfaction and loyalty.

12.2 Incorporating Mindfulness Moments throughout the Day

Incorporating mindfulness moments throughout a busy day can serve as a bridge between the fast-paced demands of work and personal well-being. This practice is not only about finding peace in stillness but also about integrating awareness into every action, fostering a sense of presence that enhances productivity and reduces stress. By embedding short, mindful pauses into our daily routines, we transform ordinary tasks into opportunities for self-care and reflection.

Mindfulness can be seamlessly woven into the fabric of our day through simple yet effective practices. These moments do not require special equipment or significant time investments but rather a deliberate intention to pause and connect with the present moment. Here are some practical ways to incorporate mindfulness into your day:

- Begin your day with intention: Start with a few minutes of quiet reflection or meditation each morning to set a positive tone for the day ahead.

- Mindful breathing: Whenever you feel overwhelmed or need to refocus, take a brief pause to concentrate solely on your breath. This can be done anywhere, anytime, helping to center your thoughts and emotions.

- Eat mindfully: Transform meals into an exercise in mindfulness by eating slowly and without distractions, savoring each bite and being fully present with the experience.

- Walking meditations: Use short walks, even if it's just around the office or during a break, as an opportunity to practice walking meditation by paying attention to the sensation of movement and your surroundings.

- Mindful listening: During conversations, practice fully focusing on the speaker without planning your response while they talk. This not only improves communication but also deepens connections with others.

Integrating these practices into daily life helps cultivate a mindful mindset that can significantly reduce stress and enhance overall well-being. It encourages us to slow down and appreciate the present moment, leading to greater clarity, decision-making skills, and emotional resilience. Moreover, by practicing mindfulness regularly, we develop a deeper connection with ourselves and our environment, promoting a balanced lifestyle amidst our busy schedules.

In conclusion, incorporating mindfulness moments throughout the day is an accessible strategy for anyone looking to improve their mental health and quality of life. These practices offer powerful tools for navigating stressors with grace and maintaining focus amidst distractions. By embracing mindfulness in daily activities, we open ourselves up to experiencing more joy, creativity, and fulfillment in every aspect of our lives.

12.3 Tips on Time Management

Time management is a crucial skill for integrating yoga and mindfulness into a busy schedule. It's about making the most of your available time to ensure that self-care and well-being are not sidelined by the demands of daily life. Effective time management allows you to carve out moments for short yoga breaks, which can significantly enhance your productivity, focus, and stress levels.

To successfully incorporate these practices into your routine, consider the following strategies:

Incorporating these tips into daily life requires commitment but the benefits are manifold. Improved time management not only facilitates the inclusion of yoga and mindfulness into a busy schedule but also enhances overall productivity and well-being. By setting clear priorities, being adaptable, and using technology wisely, finding time for self-care amidst a packed agenda becomes achievable. Embracing these practices fosters a balanced lifestyle where personal health and professional responsibilities complement rather than compete with each other.

- Prioritize your tasks: Start by identifying the most important tasks each day and allocate specific times for them. This helps in creating a structured schedule that includes slots for short yoga or mindfulness sessions.

- Use reminders: Set reminders on your phone or computer to take short breaks for mindfulness or yoga stretches. These breaks do not need to be long; even 5-10 minutes can be rejuvenating.

- Be flexible with your practice: Understand that some days will be busier than others. On extremely hectic days, it might only be feasible to fit in micro-sessions of breathing exercises or mindful walking. The key is consistency rather than duration.

- Combine activities: Integrate mindfulness into everyday activities. For instance, practice mindful eating during lunch or perform simple neck and shoulder stretches at your desk between tasks.

- Declutter digitally: Limit time spent on social media and emails during certain hours to free up more time for mindfulness and yoga practices. Digital decluttering can significantly increase available time for self-care routines.

In conclusion, managing one's time effectively is essential for maintaining balance in today's fast-paced world. By applying these strategies, individuals can ensure they are dedicating enough attention to their mental and physical health through regular yoga and mindfulness practices, ultimately leading to a more fulfilled and less stressful life.

References:

- Allen, David. "Getting Things Done: The Art of Stress-Free Productivity." This book offers insights into managing tasks and priorities to free up time for personal well-being.

- Kabat-Zinn, Jon. "Wherever You Go, There You Are: Mindfulness Meditation in Everyday Life." A guide to integrating mindfulness into daily activities, enhancing focus and relaxation.

- Covey, Stephen R. "The 7 Habits of Highly Effective People: Powerful Lessons in Personal Change." This classic book includes strategies for effective time management and setting priorities.

- Sood, Amit. "The Mayo Clinic Guide to Stress-Free Living." Provides practical advice on reducing stress through mindfulness and resilience practices.

- McGonigal, Kelly. "The Willpower Instinct: How Self-Control Works, Why It Matters, and What You Can Do to Get More of It." Offers insights into harnessing willpower for better time management and self-care.

13

Advanced Techniques for Seasoned Practitioners

13.1 Deepening Your Practice with Advanced Asanas

The journey into advanced asanas is not merely a physical endeavor but a profound exploration of the limits of body and mind, offering seasoned practitioners an opportunity to deepen their yoga practice. This progression towards more complex poses is designed to cultivate not only physical strength and flexibility but also mental resilience and spiritual growth. Advanced asanas challenge individuals to confront their perceived limitations, fostering a deeper sense of self-awareness and inner peace.

Engaging with advanced asanas requires a solid foundation in the basics of yoga, including an understanding of alignment, breath control, and body awareness. As practitioners progress, they encounter poses that demand greater balance, concentration, and discipline. These include inversions like *Adho Mukha Vrksasana* (Handstand), backbends such as *Kapotasana* (Pigeon Pose), and arm balances like *Astavakrasana* (Eight-Angle Pose). Each pose offers unique benefits, from improving cardiovascular health to enhancing digestive function, while also working to balance the energy centers within the body.

- Mental Clarity: The focus required in executing advanced poses helps clear the mind of distractions, leading to improved concentration and mental clarity.

- Emotional Resilience: By pushing through physical challenges on the mat, practitioners develop greater emotional resilience off the mat, learning to approach life's obstacles with calmness and equanimity.

- Spiritual Growth: Advanced practice often incorporates meditation and pranayama (breath work), deepening one's connection to the self and fostering a sense of unity with all beings.

Incorporating advanced asanas into one's practice is not about achieving perfect form or mastering every pose; rather, it is about embracing each moment on the mat as an opportunity for personal transformation. It encourages practitioners to listen deeply to their bodies, respect their boundaries, and celebrate their progress without attachment to outcomes. This mindful approach ensures that the journey into advanced asanas remains safe, enjoyable, and spiritually enriching.

To truly benefit from these challenging poses, it is essential for practitioners to maintain a consistent practice while seeking guidance from experienced teachers who can provide personalized adjustments and support. Additionally, integrating restorative practices such as *Savasana* (Corpse Pose) or gentle Yin Yoga sessions can help balance the intensity of advanced training with necessary periods of rest and recovery.

In conclusion, advancing one's yoga practice through complex asanas offers a pathway not only towards enhanced physical capabilities but also towards profound personal growth. It invites individuals to explore beyond their comfort zones, cultivating discipline, patience, and humility along the way. As such, deepening your practice with advanced asanas represents both a challenge and an opportunityâ€"a chance to transform your yoga journey into a holistic exploration of mind,body,and spirit.

13.2 Exploring Higher States through Meditation

Meditation, a cornerstone of spiritual practice across cultures, offers a pathway to exploring higher states of consciousness beyond the everyday experience. This journey into deeper meditative states is not just about tranquility or stress reduction; it's an exploration of the self and the universe at a profound level. Seasoned practitioners who embark on this path may discover insights into the nature of reality, experience profound inner peace, and even encounter transformative spiritual awakenings.

The pursuit of higher states through meditation requires patience, discipline, and a willingness to let go of attachment to physical sensations and mental chatter. As one delves deeper into meditation, the mind becomes quieter, allowing for an increased awareness of the present moment and a dissolution of the ego's boundaries. This can lead to experiences of unity with all that is, often described as enlightenment or cosmic consciousness in various spiritual traditions.

- Techniques for Deepening Meditation: Advanced practitioners often employ specific techniques to aid their journey into higher states. These may include focused concentration on a mantra or breath, visualization practices aimed at opening the third eye or heart chakra, and Kundalini yoga designed to awaken spiritual energy within.

- Challenges Along the Path: Exploring higher states is not without its challenges. Practitioners may encounter psychological barriers such as fear or resistance, requiring them to confront and integrate shadow aspects of themselves. Guidance from experienced teachers can be invaluable in navigating these obstacles.

- The Role of Community: While meditation is an individual practice, connecting with a community or sangha can provide support and inspiration. Sharing experiences with others on similar paths can help validate oneâ€™s experiences and encourage perseverance.

In conclusion, exploring higher states through meditation offers profound opportunities for personal transformation and spiritual growth. It invites practitioners to transcend ordinary perceptions of reality, leading to greater wisdom, compassion, and inner peace. However, this journey requires dedication and an open heart willing to explore the unknown depths of consciousness. By embracing both its challenges and rewards, individuals can unlock new dimensions of their being and experience life in its fullest expression.

13.3 Engaging with the Global Yoga Community

The global yoga community represents a vast and diverse tapestry of cultures, traditions, and practices. Engaging with this community offers seasoned practitioners an opportunity to deepen their understanding, expand their practice, and connect with like-minded individuals across the globe. This engagement can take many forms, from participating in international yoga retreats to joining online forums where ideas and experiences are shared freely.

One of the most enriching aspects of connecting with the global yoga community is the exposure to various styles and philosophies of yoga. Practitioners can learn about traditional forms such as Hatha, Ashtanga, or Kundalini directly from experienced teachers in different parts of the world. This not only enhances one's physical practice but also provides deeper insights into the spiritual and philosophical underpinnings of yoga.

- International Retreats and Workshops: Attending international retreats and workshops is a powerful way for practitioners to immerse themselves in different yoga traditions. These experiences often combine intensive practice with meditation and discussions on yogic philosophy, offering a holistic approach to personal growth.

- Online Communities: Digital platforms have made it easier than ever to connect with yogis worldwide. Online forums, social media groups, and virtual classes allow practitioners to share advice, experiences, and encouragement without geographical constraints.

- Cultural Exchange Programs: Participating in cultural exchange programs focused on yoga can provide unique insights into how different cultures interpret and integrate yoga practices into daily life. These programs often involve teaching as well as learning components, fostering mutual respect and understanding among participants from diverse backgrounds.

Beyond personal growth, engaging with the global yoga community fosters a sense of unity and collective consciousness among practitioners. It highlights the universal values at the heart of yoga—compassion, mindfulness, and interconnectedness—and reinforces the idea that despite our differences, we are all part of a larger whole seeking peace and fulfillment through our practice.

In conclusion, engaging with the global yoga community is not just about expanding one's own practice; it's about contributing to a larger dialogue that transcends borders and cultural divides. By sharing knowledge, experience, and support with fellow yogis around the world, seasoned practitioners can play an active role in nurturing this vibrant community.

References:

- International Yoga Federation. (n.d.). Retrieved from https://www.internationalyogafederation.net/

- Yoga Journal. (n.d.). Retreats. Retrieved from https://www.yogajournal.com/lifestyle/travel/retreats/

- Yoga Alliance. (n.d.). Online Workshops & Events. Retrieved from https://www.yogaalliance.org/Get_Involved/Online_Workshops_Events

- MindBodyGreen. (n.d.). Yoga. Retrieved from https://www.mindbodygreen.com/collections/yoga

- The Art of Living. (n.d.). International Yoga Day 2023: Celebrating Yoga Around the World. Retrieved from https://www.artofliving.org/international-yoga-day

14

Navigating Complex Negotiations with Clarity

14.1 Applying Mindfulness to Communication

In the realm of politics, effective communication is not merely about conveying a message but also about listening, understanding, and responding with clarity and compassion. Applying mindfulness to communication involves a conscious effort to be fully present during interactions, fostering a deeper connection between individuals. This approach can significantly enhance the quality of dialogue in political settings, where misunderstandings and conflicts are common.

Mindfulness in communication encourages individuals to listen actively without judgment or preconception, allowing for a more genuine understanding of the other party's perspective. This level of attentiveness can lead to more productive discussions and negotiations, as it promotes empathy and openness. Politicians who practice mindful communication are better equipped to address complex issues with sensitivity and insight, navigating the intricacies of political discourse with greater ease.

The application of mindfulness in communication extends beyond individual benefits; it has the potential to transform political culture by promoting respect, understanding, and cooperation among leaders. As outlined in "YOGA! FOR POLITICIANS," integrating mindfulness practices into daily routines can help politicians navigate the challenges of leadership with grace and resilience. By prioritizing mindful communication, political figures can lead more effectively, fostering environments where dialogue thrives on mutual respect and shared goals for societal progress.

- Enhancing Emotional Intelligence: Mindful communication fosters emotional intelligence by encouraging politicians to recognize their own emotions and those of others. This awareness can lead to more empathetic interactions and decisions that consider the emotional impact on all stakeholders.

- Reducing Reactivity: By staying present and focused, politicians can reduce knee-jerk reactions in stressful situations. Mindfulness helps in responding thoughtfully rather than reacting impulsively, contributing to more measured and constructive political discourse.

- Improving Public Speaking: Mindfulness techniques such as focused breathing can help manage public speaking anxiety, enabling politicians to deliver speeches with confidence and clarity. A calm demeanor enhances the speaker's credibility and the audience's receptiveness.

14.2 Strategies for Remaining Calm under Pressure

In high-stakes environments such as political negotiations, the ability to remain calm under pressure is not just a skill but a necessity. This section delves into strategies that can help individuals maintain their composure in the face of challenges, drawing from both traditional practices and modern psychological research. By integrating these approaches, politicians and negotiators can enhance their resilience and effectiveness.

Firstly, recognizing the signs of stress early on is crucial. Physical symptoms such as increased heart rate, shallow breathing, or tension in the muscles are indicators that stress levels are rising. Acknowledging these signs allows individuals to take proactive steps before their stress escalates further.

Beyond individual techniques, creating a support network is also vital. Sharing concerns with trusted colleagues or mentors can provide new perspectives and solutions to challenging situations. Additionally, learning from past experiences by reflecting on what strategies worked best under pressure can inform future responses to stress.

- Deep Breathing Techniques: One of the most immediate ways to counteract stress is through deep breathing exercises. By focusing on slow, deep breaths, individuals can activate their body's relaxation response, reducing stress hormones and calming the mind.

- Mental Rehearsal: Visualization or mental rehearsal involves running through a stressful scenario in one's mind and envisioning a positive outcome. This practice can help reduce anxiety by preparing the mind for what's to come, making the actual situation feel more manageable.

- Physical Exercise: Regular physical activity is known to reduce overall levels of tension, elevate and stabilize mood, improve sleep, and improve self-esteem. Even five minutes of aerobic exercise can stimulate anti-anxiety effects.

- Mindfulness Meditation: Building on the principles outlined in mindful communication, mindfulness meditation encourages present-moment awareness without judgment. This practice helps individuals detach from stressful thoughts and emotions, gaining a clearer perspective on the situation at hand.

In conclusion, remaining calm under pressure in political negotiations requires both preparation and practice. By incorporating these strategies into daily routines, politicians can develop greater resilience against stressors they face regularly. This not only benefits their personal well-being but also enhances their capacity to lead with clarity and decisiveness during critical moments.

14.3 Building Consensus through Compassionate Dialogue

In the realm of complex negotiations, the art of building consensus is pivotal. This process goes beyond mere agreement, seeking to unify diverse perspectives into a cohesive strategy that all parties can support. Central to this endeavor is compassionate dialogue, a communication approach that emphasizes empathy, understanding, and mutual respect. By prioritizing these values, negotiators can navigate contentious issues more effectively, fostering an environment where consensus is not just possible but probable.

Compassionate dialogue begins with active listening. This involves fully concentrating on what is being said rather than passively hearing the message of the speaker. It's about understanding the emotions and intentions behind words, which can often reveal common ground in seemingly polarized positions. Active listening also signals respect for the speaker's perspective, laying a foundation for trust and openness.

The benefits of compassionate dialogue extend beyond reaching agreement; it also enhances relationships among parties by fostering mutual respect and understanding. These strengthened relationships can prove invaluable in future negotiations, creating a more collaborative atmosphere from the outset.

- Empathy: Empathy is at the heart of compassionate dialogue. It allows negotiators to see the world from another's viewpoint, appreciating their concerns and motivations without necessarily agreeing with them. This empathetic stance can transform negotiations by shifting focus from winning an argument to solving a problem collaboratively.

- Respectful Communication: Respectful communication involves expressing thoughts and feelings in a way that respects others' dignity. It means avoiding language that might be perceived as judgmental or dismissive and instead framing messages in positive, constructive terms.

- Inclusivity: Ensuring all voices are heard is crucial for building consensus. Compassionate dialogue encourages inclusivity by actively inviting input from all stakeholders, particularly those who might otherwise be marginalized or overlooked.

In conclusion, building consensus through compassionate dialogue requires patience, empathy, and a genuine commitment to understanding others' perspectives. By incorporating these principles into negotiation strategies, individuals can navigate complex discussions more effectively, leading to outcomes that are not only satisfactory but also sustainable over time.

References:

- Rogers, C. R. (1961). On Becoming a Person: A Therapist's View of Psychotherapy. Houghton Mifflin.

- Stone, D., Patton, B., & Heen, S. (2010). Difficult Conversations: How to Discuss What Matters Most. Penguin Books.

- Fisher, R., Ury, W., & Patton, B. (2011). Getting to Yes: Negotiating Agreement Without Giving In. Penguin Books.

- Lederach, J.P. (2003). The Little Book of Conflict Transformation: Clear Articulation Of The Guiding Principles By A Pioneer In The Field. Good Books.

- Isaacs, W. (1999). Dialogue and the Art of Thinking Together: A Pioneering Approach to Communicating in Business and in Life. Currency.

15

Leading with Wisdom and Compassion

1.1 Lessons from Historical Leaders

The exploration of leadership through the lens of history offers invaluable lessons on wisdom and compassion, traits that are increasingly relevant in today's complex political landscape. By examining the lives and decisions of historical leaders, we can glean insights into how they navigated challenges with foresight, empathy, and strategic acumen. This section delves into the practices and philosophies of renowned leaders who exemplified these qualities, shedding light on how their legacies inform contemporary leadership models.

One notable figure is Mahatma Gandhi, whose commitment to non-violence and justice showcases the power of leading with a steadfast moral compass.

Gandhi's approach to political activism—emphasizing patience, understanding, and peaceful resistance—offers a blueprint for addressing conflict with dignity and respect for all parties involved. His teachings underscore the importance of inner strength and self-discipline, illustrating how personal integrity can inspire collective action and drive societal change.

Another exemplary leader is Nelson Mandela, whose resilience in the face of adversity and dedication to reconciliation in post-apartheid South Africa highlight the virtues of forgiveness and inclusivity. Mandela's ability to unite a divided nation by fostering a culture of understanding and cooperation speaks volumes about his visionary leadership. His example demonstrates how embracing our shared humanity can bridge even the deepest divides, creating pathways to peace and progress.

- Gandhi's emphasis on non-violence as a powerful tool for social change.

- Mandela's focus on reconciliation as foundational to nation-building.

- The application of wisdom and compassion in overcoming personal and political challenges.

In reflecting on these historical figures, it becomes evident that wisdom and compassion are not merely ethical considerations but strategic imperatives for effective leadership. These qualities enable leaders to navigate complexity with grace, build consensus amidst conflict, and foster environments where innovation and collaboration thrive. As we face global challenges marked by division and uncertainty, the lessons from these leaders serve as a reminder that leading with heart and mind is essential for creating a more just, peaceful, and prosperous world.

15.2 Cultivating Self-Awareness

In the journey of leadership, cultivating self-awareness stands as a cornerstone for guiding actions with wisdom and compassion. This process involves a deep dive into one's values, beliefs, and emotional triggers, enabling leaders to navigate complex situations with greater clarity and intentionality. By developing a keen understanding of oneself, leaders can foster authentic connections, make more informed decisions, and inspire trust among their followers.

Self-awareness is not an innate trait but a skill that can be developed through reflection, feedback, and mindfulness practices. It requires the willingness to confront uncomfortable truths about oneself and the humility to acknowledge personal limitations. This introspective journey allows leaders to identify their strengths and areas for growth, paving the way for continuous improvement.

- Engaging in regular self-reflection to examine one's thoughts, feelings, and behaviors.

- Seeking constructive feedback from peers, mentors, and team members to gain diverse perspectives on one's leadership style.

- Practicing mindfulness to stay present in the moment and respond rather than react during stressful situations.

Beyond personal development, cultivating self-awareness has profound implications for leadership effectiveness. It enhances emotional intelligence, which is critical for managing relationships and leading teams with empathy. Leaders who are self-aware are better equipped to handle conflicts constructively, communicate with transparency, and motivate others towards shared goals. Moreover, by modeling self-awareness, leaders can create a culture of openness and learning within their organizations.

The stories of historical figures like Gandhi and Mandela underscore the transformative power of self-awareness in leadership. Their ability to lead with integrity and influence positive change was rooted in a deep understanding of their inner selves. These examples serve as powerful reminders that true leadership emanates from within. As we navigate the complexities of modern-day leadership challenges, cultivating self-awareness remains an essential practice for anyone aspiring to lead with wisdom and compassion.

15.3 Integrating Wisdom into Decision-Making

Integrating wisdom into decision-making is a pivotal aspect of leadership that transcends mere analytical thinking. It involves the synthesis of knowledge, experience, and deep understanding to make choices that are not only effective but also ethically sound and compassionate. This integration is crucial for leaders who aim to navigate the complexities of modern organizational life, where decisions often have far-reaching implications.

Wisdom in decision-making requires a balance between cognitive intelligence and emotional intelligence. Cognitive intelligence enables leaders to analyze data, recognize patterns, and think strategically. Emotional intelligence, on the other hand, allows them to understand and manage their own emotions and those of others, fostering empathy and effective communication. The confluence of these intelligences enables leaders to consider the broader impact of their decisions, including potential effects on stakeholders' well-being and long-term organizational sustainability.

- Emphasizing ethical considerations by weighing the moral implications of decisions.

- Incorporating diverse perspectives to ensure decisions are inclusive and equitable.

- Reflecting on past experiences to draw lessons that inform current choices.

The process also involves a commitment to continuous learning. By remaining open to new information and different viewpoints, leaders can adapt their decision-making strategies as circumstances evolve. This adaptability is key in today's fast-paced world, where rigid adherence to outdated methods can lead to missed opportunities or unintended consequences.

Moreover, integrating wisdom into decision-making contributes to building a culture of trust within organizations. When employees see that decisions are made with consideration for ethical standards and their welfare, they are more likely to feel valued and respected. This fosters loyalty, motivation, and engagement among team members, driving collective success.

In conclusion, integrating wisdom into decision-making is not merely about making smart choices; it's about making right choices that advance the common good while achieving strategic objectives. Leaders who master this integration set themselves apart by creating environments where ethical considerations stand at the forefront of strategic planning and execution. As such, cultivating wisdom becomes an indispensable part of leadership development for those aspiring to lead with integrity in an increasingly complex world.

References:

- Goleman, D. (1995). Emotional Intelligence. Bantam Books. This book introduces the concept of emotional intelligence and its importance in leadership.

- Brown, B. (2018). Dare to Lead: Brave Work. Tough Conversations. Whole Hearts. Random House. BrenÃ© Brown discusses the role of courage and vulnerability in creating effective leadership.

- Schwartz, T., Gomes, J., & McCarthy, C. (2010). The Way We're Working Isn't Working: The Four Forgotten Needs That Energize Great Performance. Free Press. This work explores how leaders can improve performance by addressing physical, emotional, mental, and spiritual needs.

- Kidder, R.M. (2009). How Good People Make Tough Choices: Resolving the Dilemmas of Ethical Living. Harper Perennial. Kidder offers insights into making ethical decisions in complex situations.

- Heifetz, R.A., Linsky, M., & Grashow, A. (2009). The Practice of Adaptive Leadership: Tools and Tactics for

Changing Your Organization and the World. Harvard Business Press. This book provides strategies for leaders to adapt to changing environments and make wise decisions.

16

Ethical Leadership in Times of Crisis

16.1 Responding to Crisis with Mindfulness

In the realm of political leadership, crises are inevitable. They come in various forms, from natural disasters to economic downturns and political unrest. The way leaders respond to such crises can significantly impact their effectiveness and the well-being of those they serve. This is where mindfulness, a core component of yoga practice, becomes invaluable. Mindfulness in crisis management is not just about remaining calm; it's about harnessing clarity, compassion, and precision in decision-making.

Mindfulness practices enable leaders to navigate the stormy waters of crisis with a steady hand and a clear mind. By focusing on the present moment without judgment, leaders can better assess situations as they unfold, making decisions that are informed rather than reactive. This approach fosters resilience, both personally and within the organizations or communities they lead.

- Enhanced Clarity: Mindful meditation sharpens focus and clears mental clutter, allowing leaders to see through the chaos of crisis and identify viable solutions.

- Emotional Regulation: Regular mindfulness practice helps manage stress responses and regulate emotions, which is crucial in high-pressure situations where emotional reactivity can cloud judgment.

- Compassionate Leadership: By cultivating empathy through mindfulness, leaders can make more inclusive decisions that consider the well-being of all stakeholders.

Incorporating mindfulness into daily routines doesn't require extensive time commitments or drastic changes in lifestyle. Simple practices like focused breathing exercises before important meetings or mindful walking during breaks can make a significant difference in a leader's ability to respond effectively to crises.

The application of mindfulness in times of crisis extends beyond personal practice; it influences organizational culture and decision-making processes. Leaders who embody mindful practices inspire their teams to adopt similar approaches, leading to a more resilient organization capable of weathering challenges with grace and agility.

In conclusion, responding to crisis with mindfulness offers political leaders a powerful tool for enhancing their leadership capabilities. It equips them with the skills needed to lead with integrity, compassion, and clarity amidst uncertainty. As outlined in "YOGA! FOR POLITICIANS," integrating yoga's principles into political leadership not only benefits individual leaders but also has the potential to transform governance for the greater good.

16.2 Maintaining Integrity in Turbulent Times

In the face of adversity, maintaining integrity is both a challenge and a necessity for leaders. Turbulent times often test the moral compass of individuals in leadership positions, pushing them to make difficult decisions that can have far-reaching consequences. The essence of integrity lies in consistency between one's values, words, and actions, even when such alignment comes at a cost. This section delves into the importance of upholding integrity during crises and provides insights into how leaders can navigate these challenges effectively.

Crises can distort the usual parameters for decision-making, presenting ethical dilemmas that are not easily navigated with standard protocols. In such scenarios, the temptation to compromise on principles for short-term gains or out of fear can be overwhelming. However, it is precisely in these moments that integrity becomes most critical. Leaders who maintain their ethical standards serve as beacons of trust and stability, fostering resilience within their organizations or communities.

Maintaining integrity in turbulent times requires a deep understanding of one's core values and a steadfast commitment to acting in accordance with those values. It involves making hard choices that may not always be popular but are necessary for sustaining long-term trust and respect among stakeholders. Leaders who navigate crises with integrity inspire loyalty, drive positive change, and build stronger, more resilient organizations capable of withstanding future challenges.

- Transparent Communication: Openness in communication fosters trust and credibility. Leaders should strive to be honest about the situation's realities while also conveying hope and a clear plan for navigating through the crisis.

- Accountability: Taking responsibility for decisions is fundamental to integrity. Acknowledging mistakes and learning from them demonstrates humility and commitment to ethical leadership.

- Ethical Decision-Making: When faced with tough choices, ethical leaders weigh the consequences of their actions on all stakeholders. They prioritize fairness, justice, and the greater good over personal or organizational gain.

In conclusion, while crises inevitably bring uncertainty and disruption, they also present opportunities for leaders to demonstrate true leadership through integrity. By adhering to ethical principles and leading by example, leaders can guide their teams through adversity with confidence and emerge stronger on the other side.

16.3 Leading with Empathy and Compassion

In the labyrinth of leadership challenges, steering through crises demands not just strategic acumen but a profound sense of empathy and compassion. This section delves into the pivotal role these human-centric qualities play in guiding teams and organizations through turbulent times. Empathy and compassion are not mere soft skills but essential leadership tools that can significantly influence an organization's resilience and recovery trajectory.

Empathy, the ability to understand and share the feelings of another, becomes particularly crucial during crises. It enables leaders to gauge the emotional state and needs of their team members, fostering a supportive environment that encourages open communication and mutual support. Compassionate leadership goes a step further by not only recognizing pain or stress in others but also taking action to alleviate it. Together, empathy and compassion create a foundation for trust, which is indispensable in times of uncertainty.

The impact of leading with empathy and compassion extends beyond immediate crisis management. These qualities help in building more cohesive teams that are better equipped to navigate future challenges. Moreover, empathetic leadership promotes a culture of inclusivity where diverse perspectives are valued and leveraged for creative solutions.

- Building Trust Through Vulnerability: Leaders who demonstrate vulnerability by sharing their own concerns or uncertainties can strengthen connections with their team members, making it easier for others to express their fears or challenges without fear of judgment.

- Active Listening: Empathetic leaders prioritize listening over speaking. By actively listening to their team's worries, suggestions, and feedback, leaders can make informed decisions that reflect the collective insights and needs of their organization.

- Promoting Psychological Safety: Creating an environment where individuals feel safe to voice their opinions, ask questions, or admit mistakes without fear of retribution is crucial during crises. This psychological safety encourages innovation, adaptability, and problem-solving.

In conclusion, empathy and compassion are indispensable qualities for effective leadership in times of crisis. By prioritizing these values, leaders can inspire loyalty, foster resilience, and pave the way for sustainable recovery and growth. The true measure of a leader is often revealed not in moments of comfort but in how they respond to adversity—leading with empathy and compassion is a testament to one's commitment to ethical leadership.

References:

- Brown, Brené. "Dare to Lead: Brave Work. Tough Conversations. Whole Hearts." Random House, 2018.This book emphasizes the importance of vulnerability and courage in leadership, advocating for empathy and connection as foundational to leading effectively.

- Edmondson, Amy C. "The Fearless Organization: Creating Psychological Safety in the Workplace for Learning, Innovation, and Growth." Wiley, 2019.Edmondson's work highlights the critical role of psychological safety in fostering an innovative and inclusive workplace culture.

- George, Bill. "True North: Discover Your Authentic Leadership." Jossey-Bass, 2007.George explores authentic leadership and its reliance on understanding oneself and leading with empathy to build strong organizations.

- Goleman, Daniel. "Primal Leadership: Unleashing the Power of Emotional Intelligence." Harvard Business Review Press, 2013.Goleman discusses how emotional intelligence shapes effective leaders who can resonate with others' emotions to drive positive outcomes.

17

Towards a Future of Sustainable Leadership

17.1 Envisioning a New Era of Governance

In the quest for sustainable leadership, envisioning a new era of governance emerges as a pivotal theme. This vision is not just about altering policies or introducing reforms; it's about fundamentally rethinking the role of leaders in society and how they connect with their constituents. The integration of practices like yoga into the daily routines of politicians can serve as a cornerstone for this transformation, offering a pathway to enhanced mental clarity, emotional resilience, and physical stamina.

The importance of this shift cannot be overstated. In an age where political landscapes are increasingly volatile and public trust is at a premium, the need for leaders who are not only effective but also grounded and mindful has never been more critical. Yoga, with its holistic approach to well-being, offers tools that can help leaders navigate these challenges with grace and integrity.

- Stress Reduction: Yoga's proven benefits in stress management can help politicians cope with the high-pressure demands of their roles.

- Improved Decision-Making: By enhancing mental clarity, yoga practices enable leaders to make more thoughtful and considered decisions.

- Emotional Resilience: Regular engagement with yoga can bolster emotional strength, allowing leaders to maintain their composure in challenging situations.

- Physical Stamina: The physical aspects of yoga ensure that leaders remain energized and capable of meeting the rigorous demands of their schedules.

Beyond individual benefits, envisioning a new era of governance also involves creating cultures within political institutions that prioritize wellness and ethical alignment. Incorporating yoga into governmental organizations could foster environments where teamwork, compassion, and integrity flourish. This cultural shift could significantly reduce burnout rates among staff members while building leadership structures resilient enough to face contemporary challenges head-on.

In conclusion, as we stand on the cusp of this new era in governance, it becomes clear that sustainable leadership requires more than just strategic acumen or political savvy. It necessitates a holistic approach to personal development and organizational cultureâ€"one where practices like yoga play an integral role in shaping leaders who are not only effective but also balanced, ethical, and compassionate. This vision for governance holds the promise of transforming political leadership into a force for positive change in the 21st century.

17.2 Integrating Yoga into Political Culture

The integration of yoga into political culture represents a transformative approach to governance, aiming to cultivate leaders who embody mindfulness, resilience, and ethical decision-making. This initiative is not merely about adding a physical regimen to the daily schedule of politicians but embedding a philosophy that promotes holistic well-being, emotional intelligence, and compassionate leadership.

Yoga's ancient practice offers more than physical benefits; it provides mental clarity and emotional balance, essential qualities for those in the demanding realm of politics. By adopting yoga, political leaders can enhance their ability to remain focused and calm amidst crises, improving their capacity to lead with empathy and foresight. The practice encourages a mindset that values patience, understanding, and respect for diverse perspectivesâ€"traits increasingly necessary in todayâ€™s polarized political environments.

Incorporating yoga into political culture also has broader implications for societal well-being. When leaders exhibit balance, integrity, and compassionâ€"qualities nurtured through yogaâ€"they set a positive example for citizens and encourage a more harmonious society. Moreover, by prioritizing mental health and ethical conduct in governance structures themselves, institutions can become beacons of stability and trustworthiness in an era marked by uncertainty.

- Enhancing Emotional Intelligence: Regular yoga practice helps in recognizing one's own emotions as well as those of others, fostering empathy and better communication between leaders and constituents.

- Cultivating Mindfulness: Through meditation and focused breathing exercises, yoga assists leaders in developing a heightened awareness of the present moment, enabling more deliberate and thoughtful responses to challenges.

- Promoting Physical Health: The physical postures (asanas) improve stamina, flexibility, and overall health, ensuring that leaders are physically prepared to endure the rigors of their positions.

- Building Resilient Leadership: Yoga's emphasis on inner peace and contentment equips leaders with the resilience needed to navigate the complexities of governance without succumbing to stress or burnout.

In conclusion, integrating yoga into political culture is not just an innovative approach to personal development for politicians; it's a strategic investment in the future of governance. As we move towards creating sustainable leadership models capable of addressing 21st-century challenges head-on, embracing practices like yoga could very well be the key to nurturing leaders who are not only effective but truly inspirational.

17.3 Creating a Legacy of Wisdom and Compassion

The concept of creating a legacy of wisdom and compassion is pivotal in the journey towards sustainable leadership. This approach transcends traditional leadership paradigms by emphasizing the cultivation of deep, intrinsic values that benefit not only the leader but society as a whole. In this context, wisdom refers to the ability to make decisions based on a profound understanding of human nature, societal needs, and environmental considerations. Compassion involves a genuine empathy for others' suffering and a commitment to action aimed at alleviating it.

Wisdom and compassion as foundational pillars enable leaders to navigate complex challenges with foresight and humanity. These qualities ensure that decision-making processes are not solely driven by short-term gains or personal ambitions but are informed by a long-term vision for societal well-being and global sustainability. The integration of these values into leadership practices can transform organizational cultures, inspire teams, and lead to more ethical and effective governance models.

In practice, creating a legacy of wisdom and compassion involves continuous self-reflection, learning from diverse sources of knowledge, engaging in meaningful dialogues with various stakeholders, and committing to personal growth that aligns with these values. It also requires courage to challenge prevailing norms and innovate new paths forward that prioritize collective well-being over individual success.

- Empowering Ethical Leadership: Leaders who embody wisdom and compassion naturally prioritize ethical considerations in their decision-making processes, setting standards for integrity and accountability within their organizations.

- Fostering Inclusive Communities: By leading with empathy, such leaders create environments where diversity is valued, different perspectives are welcomed, and everyone feels respected and included.

- Enhancing Resilience: Wisdom enables leaders to anticipate future challenges and prepare accordingly, while compassion ensures that they remain connected to the needs of their people, fostering resilience in the face of adversity.

In conclusion, as we envision the future of leadership in an increasingly complex world, embedding wisdom and compassion into the core of leadership practices offers a transformative pathway towards achieving sustainable development goals. It not only enhances the effectiveness of leaders but also contributes significantly to building more just, peaceful, and resilient societies.

References:

- Northouse, P. G. (2018). Leadership: Theory and Practice. Sage Publications. This book provides a comprehensive overview of various leadership theories, including ethical leadership models that emphasize wisdom and compassion.

- Kanov, J., Maitlis, S., Worline, M. C., Dutton, J. E., Frost, P. J., & Lilius, J. M. (2004). Compassion in Organizational Life. American Behavioral Scientist,

47(6), 808-827.This article explores the role of compassion in enhancing organizational effectiveness and fostering positive workplace environments.

- Senge, P. (1990). The Fifth Discipline: The Art & Practice of The Learning Organization. Currency Doubleday. Senge's work on systems thinking and learning organizations highlights the importance of wisdom in navigating complex challenges and creating sustainable solutions.

- George, B., Sims, P., McLean, A.N., & Mayer, D. (2007). Discovering Your Authentic Leadership. Harvard Business Review. This article discusses how authentic leadership grounded in personal values such as wisdom and compassion can inspire trust and loyalty among followers.

"YOGA! FOR POLITICIANS" is a pioneering guide that introduces yoga as an essential tool for political leaders grappling with the stresses and demands of their roles. This non-fiction book highlights the importance of mental clarity, emotional resilience, and physical stamina for those in the political sphere, offering yoga as a means to achieve these qualities. The work is designed to be accessible to both experienced yogis and beginners, providing practical advice on incorporating yoga practices into the hectic schedules of politicians.

The book begins by presenting research on how yoga can reduce stress, enhance decision-making capabilities, and improve overall well-being. It then explores how these benefits apply specifically to political life, addressing challenges such as public speaking anxiety and the need for empathy and patience in legislative processes. Through targeted strategies, including poses, breathing exercises, and meditation practices, it aims to help political figures find balance in both their personal and professional lives.

One of the notable insights is the concept of "ethical alignment," which draws parallels between yoga's ethical precepts and good governance principles. The book argues that integrating yoga into daily routines can promote integrity, transparency, and accountability in public service. Additionally, it advocates for incorporating yoga programs within governmental organizations to foster team cohesion, reduce burnout rates among staff members, and build resilient leadership structures.

Overall, "YOGA! FOR POLITICIANS" serves as a comprehensive resource for anyone involved in governance seeking to lead with strength, wisdom, and compassion. It underscores the transformative power of aligning mind, body, and spirit not only for personal betterment but also for the greater good.